Put On Your

A practical guide tc ...ing ..c....c., ..appier and
more successful in 52 weekly steps

PUT ON YOUR OWN OXYGEN MASK FIRST

A PRACTICAL GUIDE TO LIVING HEALTHIER, HAPPIER AND MORE SUCCESSFUL IN 52 WEEKS

Alfons and Ulrike Staerk
www.KeruUmaBudo.com

First Edition

ABOUT THIS BOOK

Much of what you will read stems from martial arts lessons and strategies I learned in business. A significant contribution also comes from my wife Uli and her thoughts on minimalism, simplification, the arts, and focusing on experiences rather than material possessions.

None of what you will read is rocket science or my own discovery. However, it is a summary of principles and approaches that worked for me over the past 25 years, leaving out all the things that I learned the hard way not to work. Those principles helped me stay sane and healthy in environments of extreme challenge and pressure.

Pictures and illustrations are either copyright of Alfons and Ulrike Staerk or shared under Creative Commons CC0 from Pixabay. Pictures in the foreword are copyright of Thomas Aschenbrenner.

To Thomas Aschenbrenner, who was my manager many years ago. He had faith and granted me responsibility for my first team. He set in motion my professional journey.

To Hilmar Fuchs, our friend and Tai Chi teacher, who taught us life priorities and to always have fun. He served as our role model through the years, always putting family first, health second, and everything else after that. Without his example and teachings, I would have burned out many years ago.

To our parents, who provided the resources and encouragement to study, learn, and set our goals and ambitions high. They will always be role models for us.

To our colleagues and team members who accepted our mistakes, gave us patiently feedback until we 'got it', and helped us learn and grow.

To our kids who not always saw Dad as often as they should have. We hope they will build on our good examples while improving on our flaws.

CONTENTS

INTRODUCTION

Life is a marathon, not a sprint.

FOREWORD

Thomas was my manager 15 years ago when he took the massive leap of faith to entrust his team to a passionate but completely untested individual as their new manager. That inexperienced and untested individual was me.

Thomas' faith and willingness to take a risk has set me up on my professional path as a manager, and as such, enabled many of the learnings I share in this book. Given that Thomas has set in motion my management path, and with that a whole new world of exciting and often unexpected learnings, I am incredibly proud that he volunteered to write this foreword.

The learnings in this book come from many different situations and mentors. However, Thomas was the one who has pointed me in the right direction and then sent me out to explore.

We are still in contact after all those years and follow each other's lives, albeit now on different continents. We still share many of the same thoughts and values, and it is a great honor for me to present his foreword.

WE ALL ARE DIFFERENT, YET ALSO THE SAME

Alfons and I have known each other for close to 25 years. We both worked in Product Marketing at Microsoft Germany. Alfons was the Technical Evangelist and Lead for Windows, while I led Product Marketing across the company.

It was an exciting and thrilling time. PCs were spreading into all areas of life; the software industry was growing extremely fast, being the driver of that change. Everyone believed in the computer revolution and lived that passion every day.

Alfons and I – we were similar, yet very different. He was a calm, thoughtful person. At times, I felt he consciously held himself back, while always projecting a definite presence and inner strength. Even back then, I perceived this unique presence very positive and appropriate, never regarding it as passive – and this in a business environment, where one always thinks that things need to be 'pushed,' 'driven,' or 'disrupted.'

On the other hand, I was more of a front man, an initiator, an activator; at times maybe a little too much… I was energized, charged, and most times, that was very evident for my team and environment. I am aware that as a very extrovert person with all the passion and excitement one can, at times, shoot over the target. That surely happened to me back in the day and still happens today. I hope in the end this energy was still predominantly ok and positive. I had lots of ideas, lots of energy, lots of adrenalin, and always an abundance of motivation. I still have lots of ideas, energy, and motivation today. However, luckily, I liberated myself from adrenalin as a daily drug more and more.

For many years now, Alfons and I live separated by a distance of more than 5,000 miles, having only limited personal contact. However, in many ways, I think we are even closer today than we were back then. I find that very curious but also enjoyable. At first glance, we are 'connected' through social media, like everyone else. However, this is not comparing 'my latest car, house, family, vacation' like it so often happens. There is a much stronger similarity and connection in how we live our careers and lives, how we find strength, energy, and motivation and from where we get our **oxygen**.

What's connecting us is not the tool or the platform, like Facebook, LinkedIn, or Instagram. It is how we look at life itself, its opportunities but also its challenges. It's about shared experiences and values. For both of us, a successful and meaningful career is still an essential part of our lives. However, it's only one side, and maybe just the result of a deeper connection to more fundamental interests and resources that we both share and find in ourselves: nature, sports, exercise, reflection, calmness and most of all family. We both live a conscious life in harmony with family and nature.

These views connect us despite any intercontinental distances, and I am sure many of you enjoy similar experiences and connections. They will be different for every one of us, but those connections are more important than job, career or money. Alfons and Uli draw many of their values from the clear and wise structures and principles of Asian martial arts and culture. For me, it is mainly music, the mountains, and lots of exercise in nature. Ten years ago, I made a conscious decision to leave our beautiful house in the city, and move into the country with my family. We put a lot of personal time and energy in renovating a 100-year-old farm in the beautiful Allgaeu area in southern Germany. There we are living in the heart of nature, with horses, the breathtaking mountains close by, lakes abound and gorgeous scenery everywhere.

I'm part hobby-farmer and part still manager and entrepreneur. Just now, in summer 2019, we brought in hay – a lot of work in 100 degrees heat on the field. While that lifestyle might seem schizophrenic at first glance, it taught me a lot while also giving me a lot back, mainly calmness, balance, and grounding. Others might find those stimulations through reading, yoga, gardening, cooking, sailing, fishing – it doesn't matter what.

The important thing is that you identify such stimulations for your inner values and passions and that you activate and live them. I think Alfons and Uli found the keys to those doors and used them as a source of energy even earlier than I could. However, the when and how is not the key. Instead, it is critical that you discover for yourself what those energy sources and passions are. Then all you need to do is to find and walk the path, to live and leverage them. Once you connect with and leverage those sources, you will find that things suddenly get better, seem more intuitive, more natural, and opportunities manifest themselves.

On the flip side, countless drains in our lives are continuously trying to pull that newfound energy and positive attitude away from us. We need also to pay attention to those drains and aim to control, limit, and avoid them. Examples for such drains are too much work (too many hours), unhealthy and processed food, lack of sleep, permanent stress and multitasking, not enough exercise, continuous distraction through media, TV, etc…

You will read about many of these sources and drains in this book, while also finding excellent tips and suggestions on how to manage them. Decide and pick the ones that are working best and are most meaningful for you. It's critical to be clear, that the goal is not to structure, plan, and optimize every minute of your life. You can do that if that's your style and preference, but you don't have to. With this book, Alfons and Uli offer a plan in simple weekly steps and short, clear chapters that can be readily applied. Look at those suggestions as a menu, a selection, an offering of ideas, impulses, and opportunities that are both simple and proven over time.

I tend to pick things at the moment, as I see them fit my current life situation or specific challenge, stitch them together on the spot, and then try to implement them in a very hands-on way. Others will prefer to develop their own clear plan and approach. Everything is right. Everything is ok. Everything works – make it work for you!

The key is to do it and to find the right balance. The same is true for deliberately doing nothing.

> "There are only two days in the year that nothing can be done. One is called yesterday, and the other is called tomorrow, so today is the right day to love, believe, do, and mostly live."
> Dalai Lama

I hope you will enjoy this straightforward, beautiful and inspiring book. I feel honored that Alfons and Uli asked me to share my thoughts in this foreword.

> The world is changing through us.
> We change through us.
> We all change the world – a little bit every day.

Thomas Aschenbrenner
Germany, 2019

Thomas lives with his family, wife, daughter, and horses in a 100-year-old farm, which they lovingly renovated, in Allgaeu, Germany. In his business life, Thomas serves as an experienced and successful Manager and Leader in the IT and telecommunications industry for over 20 years. He is passionate about nature, environment, and creativity. Thomas' wife is a licensed Social Counselor and Horseback Riding Therapist. In that capacity, she helps children, juveniles, and adults through therapeutic riding and horsemanship to overcome problems and personal crisis as well as learning and concentration disorders.

https://www.linkedin.com/in/taschenbrenner/
http://www.fliederbachhof.de/

PREFACE

LIVE HAPPIER, HEALTHIER AND MORE SUCCESSFUL IN 52 WEEKLY STEPS

At many points in my professional life, I felt challenged to 'go all in' and sacrifice family, health, or my personal passions for success at work. Not that I was asked to do it, but I thought I had to. Luckily, I caught these imbalances early enough to avoid going down on a doom spiral. I started to pay close attention to principles and methods that helped me be more efficient and allowed me to have both a great professional career as well as a healthy and fulfilling personal life.

Live is a marathon, not a sprint.

Our lives must be balanced to have sustainable success and fulfillment. In this book, I want to share the principles that helped me achieve that balance. Those principles and methods are based on scientific research as well as what I learned from mentors and role models at work and in my personal life.

I will spare reciting scientific studies; there are plenty of books out there and many pages already filled with going in the details. Instead, I aim to provide a no-nonsense practical guide of things that have worked for me.

Any change in behavior requires a change in habits, and those are hard. To help develop new habits, I have organized the first part of this book into a series of 52 specific changes. Pick one every week and add to it. You might go faster if you already have a particular habit or slow down if a particular practice refuses to stick. Take your time and make it work for you.

Much of what you will read stems from martial arts lessons and strategies I learned in business. A significant contribution also comes from my wife Uli and her thoughts on minimalism, simplification, the arts, and focusing on experiences rather than material possessions.

None of what you will read is rocket science or my own discovery. However, it is a summary of principles and approaches that worked for me over the past 25 years, leaving out all the things that I learned the hard way not to work. Those principles helped me stay sane and healthy in environments of extreme challenge and pressure.

PUT ON YOUR OWN OXYGEN MASK FIRST

When you travel on any commercial airplane, you will need to go through the safety briefing before taking off. One of the things that stuck with me was the advice to "put on your own oxygen mask first."

Put on your own oxygen mask first.

It seems to go against our instincts initially. We want to help our kids or the elderly before we turn our attention to our own needs. However, that is shortsighted. Even as we desire to help others, we first need to take care of ourselves.

Let me repeat this – before we can help others, we need to take care of ourselves first!

This is how this book will start. We will go from the ground up, starting with habits that improve your health and physical wellbeing. Being healthy is the basis for everything. From there on we will take it to higher levels.

However, always remember: you need to get yourself into the right place first before you can have a positive impact on your work, the people you care about and society.

Remember Maslow's hierarchy of needs and start from the bottom up.

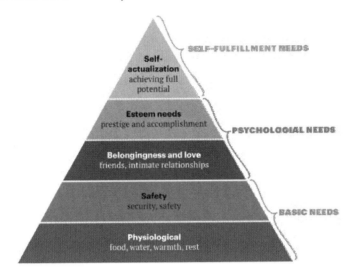

HOW THIS BOOK IS ORGANIZED

Whether you plan to read through the whole book once and then come back to tackle the things that resonate with you or you plan to go week by week and chapter by chapter, here is what awaits you.

> Take control of your life. Start your path to a healthier and more balanced life.

This book is structured in four parts. The first three present a plan for weekly habits to add to your portfolio, the fourth is a reflection on general learnings and methods to achieve your goals at work and in life.

Part I – Healthy Habits

Health comes first. Always. This section of the book will talk about fundamental changes to your lifestyle that will make sure you stay in the optimal physical shape to achieve your life goals. Moreover, that you live to experience them.

Part II – Be More Effective

The second part is about becoming more productive. We want to achieve our goals, but we want to do that within reasonable time limits. We don't want to waste time at work; we want to achieve things right away. Ultimately this will free up time to follow our personal passions and spirituality.

Part III – Spiritual Balance

Life is about more than work and a healthy body. It is about the things we care about, our families, friends, and passions. We have learned to make room in our lives in the previous sections; in this section, we will explore how we can fill that room in the most meaningful way.

Part IV – Reflections on Achieving Your Goals

The last section in the book will close by examining broader principles that will help us identify and achieve our goals. The topics in this section are more extensive and not as conducive to be picked up as a habit in a given week. Take them as food for reflections and apply them when the opportunity presents itself.

WHERE WILL YOU GO?

After you have read this book, you will need to decide where YOU want to go. What suggestions do you want to pick up? Which ones don't work for you? Feel empowered to discard them.

> "The teacher shows the door. The student decides if she will walk through it."
> Martial arts proverb

Chart your OWN course!

Alfons
Carnation, WA, 2019

ABOUT THE AUTHORS

ALFONS STAERK

Alfons worked at Hewlett Packard, Microsoft and Amazon in Executive and Senior leadership roles for the last 25 years. He has also studied various martial arts over the same period. As time progressed those worlds and the learnings from both merged for him and enriched each other. When he became a parent, a whole new world of insights opened up.

Alfons just recently found himself in a downward spiral where he neglected both his health, as well as his passions for his demanding work. Once noticed, he embarked on a deliberate journey to get his life back into a balanced and sustainable state. The first sections of is book loosely reflect that journey.

https://www.linkedin.com/in/AlfonsStaerk/

ULRIKE (ULI) STAERK

Uli is a well–known Tai Chi and Ikebana teacher in her local community.

She serves as a staff teacher for 'Mindfulness for Kids' at the local Elementary school, where she also leads the PTSA art docent program. Before moving to the US, Uli practiced as Medical Doctor at the University of Aachen in Germany.

Uli always keeps her family on track to spend time on their passions, art, and experiences. She strives to simplify life and follow a minimalist style, although it doesn't always work. She is a thoughtful food and health enthusiast and the healthy consciousness for her family. Her views on experiences and passions and ultimately on what really matters in life were invaluable for this book.

https://www.linkedin.com/in/UliStaerk/

PART I
HEALTHY HABITS

Your body is your tool. Keep it sharp!

WEEK 1:
STAY HYDRATED

L et's start building up; bottom to top. In Chinese medicine, earth and water are first, then fire and air.

Drink lots of water, stay hydrated. Keep your energy at high levels with the right fuel. Stave off colds.

It is recommended to drink between half an ounce and an ounce of water for each pound you weigh, every day. Food and other fluids contribute to the daily total. How about we shoot for three bottles of water a day?

Drink at least three bottles of water a day!

Our body consists of 60% of water. If we don't drink, we die. Water is the first step.

WEEK 2:
A STRONG CORE FOR A CONFIDENT LIFE

Aerobics is great. Tai Chi is great. Mindfulness is great. We love practicing it all regularly. However, you also need a strong core, and it makes sense to add some focused workout to develop your core strength.

A stronger core will make many activities in daily life easier for you. A stronger core is the root of any force we need to exert. A stronger core will lead to a leaner body.

A stronger core will make you more confident.

More is better, but let's start short and simple and actually do it every day (you can always do more if you have more time). Let's do these every day:

- 10 push–ups
- 20 sit-ups
- 30 secs plank

Strengthen your core. Then take it from there.

WEEK 3:
DON'T WASTE TIME IN THE MORNING

D on't start your day on the wrong foot. Stop procrastinating before tackling the day ahead. Get up and get into the right mode.

When we have a slow start, we often get frustrated with ourselves, which sends us off into a downward spiral for the rest of the day.

On the other hand, on days where we have an early and success-ful running start, we usually carry over that energy through the day. On those evenings, we tend to look back at successful and fulfilled days.

Don't waste time in the morning. There are many ways to waste time in the morning – Facebook, news, gossip, snoozing the alarm clock. None of them is helpful. Before you snooze the alarm, rather sleep longer. In-stead of wasting time on Facebook, get started with your day, end earlier, and have some time left for your family.

The same applies in the evening. Rather than dozing off in front of the TV, instead spend time with your family, read a good book or just go to bed.

The same applies to games. When did you ever truly feel better after having spent 30 mins with a video game?

> Don't waste time in the morning. Sleep or get up, but don't procrastinate in bed or on the sofa.

Ditch Facebook, news, and games. Instead do some Tai Chi, exercise, or just a quiet reflection of the day to come.

Get up and get going!

WEEK 4:
GO TO BED EARLY

Feeling tired and low in energy? How long did you sleep last night? How long the nights before?

There was a time when we bragged about how little sleep we need and how short time we can afford it because we are so busy.

We are past that. Science has proven that proper and consistent sleep is critical for physical and mental health. Not having time to sleep is more a sign of lousy prioritization than anything else (ok, if you have a newborn you get a pass on this rule).

Find a routine to go to bed at the same time every single day. Get up in the morning at the same time every day. Find out how many hours of sleep you need per night and then plan your day around that. Make it a habit.

> Go to bed early. Get up early the next morning. Establish a routine around the times when you go to bed and wake up and then stick to it.

Energized days are better days. You will get more done, which will give you more opportunity to establish free times.

On the flip side, if you don't sleep enough, you will have low energy throughout the day. Coffee cannot truly fix that. Your mind will be slow. You will be cranky and have short fuses. In one word, your day will not be productive, and you will need more time to get things done. That will cut in your remaining regeneration and sleep time – you see the vicious cycle.

It would be best if you also avoid things that get you too excited: blue lights trigger awakeness, TV gets you excited and aroused, computer games are designed to trigger your excitement and attention, checking your email one last time will almost certainly make you think about work the whole night.

Get a good (maybe slightly boring) book to read and put it away the same time every night.

For most people 8 hours sleep a night is the right duration. It seems to work for me. Find out how much sleep makes you most effective.

WEEK 5:
SKIP ALCOHOL

I love my glass of wine in the evening after a long, often exhausting but hopefully successful day. I really do. However, I have cut back on it and skipped any alcohol on workdays.

There is much debate as to whether a single glass of wine in the evening is helping or harming your health. As with any nutrition advice, the science data and recommendations change about twice a year.

What I do think it does is to impact the quality of your sleep negatively. Moderate amounts of alcohol help us to fall asleep, but they don't really lead to a good and deep sleep throughout the night.

More than one glass is bad for your health and brain anyway; there is little debate on that.

> Skip the evening drink for better sleep and better health.

Limit drinking alcohol to one glass of wine on Fridays and Saturdays only. As tempting as drinks might be after a long day, go for green tea instead. Sleep better, be sharper the next day.

WEEK 6:
CUT DOWN ON SUGAR AND SALT

We all eat too much sugar. Way too much.

Moreover, the scary part is that most times, we don't even notice or know. Sugar is in sweets (naturally), in candy (of course), but also in soda (easy to forget) and pretty much all other processed foods.

There is so much sugar in everything that our taste buds got used to it and don't even notice it anymore. When we moved over from

Germany more than ten years ago, we first couldn't eat any sweets or cookies because everything was appallingly sweet. We still skip most store cookies, but it's scary how quickly you can get used to too much sugar and won't even notice it anymore. We just have to look at our kids to see living examples of a whole different sugar perception.

Sugar gives you a quick rush and then a big and deep crash. Moreover, long-term it harms your health in many ways.

Try to stay away from things that have lots of sugar added. Once you do it, your sensibility for tastes will come back again, and you will sense sweetness even without crazy amounts of sugar. Drink your coffee without sugar, and if you don't like it that way, maybe you don't like coffee in the first place.

Rather than 'sweetening' your life with sugar (or even worse, artificial sweeteners) go for things that provide you with slow-burning glucose to give you energy for the day and keep up your willpower (we'll talk about that in a few weeks).

Moreover, while we're at it – cut down dramatically on salt. Again, almost all processed food has way too much salt in it. Sugar, salt, and fat make for great (i.e., strong) taste. They don't help you at all to get consistent energy or have healthy nutrition.

> Skip sugar, sweetener, and soda. Go for nuts,
> veggies, fruit and infused water or tea instead.
> Ditch the salt and add some pepper to your life.

Uli always uses only half of the sugar (sometimes less) that is called out in recipes. We don't drink any soft drinks (they are way too sugary, I cannot even stand the taste). We replace most of the salt with pepper. It may be a big step initially, but you will get used to it in just a few weeks, and a whole universe of new, more natural and subtle tastes will open up for you.

WEEK 7:
MAKE YOUR DIET PERSONAL

I'm a scientist at heart. Way back, I studied physics and got my masters in it. The scientific thinking stayed with me as did the urge to explain things with data, observations, and principles instead of beliefs. However, science (and scientific history) has also taught me to be careful with what we 'know to  be true.' It turned out after all that the earth is neither flat nor the center of the universe. Bummer.

There is a new diet every year that claims to have found the right way to eat finally. It's always proven through scientific studies and better than anything we had before. Funny enough the next year it will be proven wrong. It's also interesting to note that humans survived just fine for eons before we had scientific diets.

I would urge you to take ownership of your nutrition instead of just following the latest craze. Watch what you're eating and then listen to your body. What gives you energy without a feeling of fullness or being bloated. What gets you going instead of making you tired after eating.

Diet is universal for the most part but in the details also personal to your body, lifestyle, and goals. Learn what YOU need. Learn what helps

YOUR body. No one else can give you the magic recipe, not even scientists.

Take some clues from our ancestors. They thrived and put us into this world, after all. Don't go for extreme one-sided diets (I could name a bunch but I won't). Look for balance and variety. Don't be a one–trick pony. Avoid processed food whenever you can; there's little food left in there.

Many of the longest–living populations follow the same pattern: a variety of different foods, freshly cooked and seasonally adjusted. You can take clues from the Mediterranean, Japanese, or Chinese five elements nutrition (sorry, the Chinese restaurant's menu doesn't count).

Take a balanced, fresh selection as a basis and then learn what works for you.

For example, I observed that

- A lite and healthy lunch (soup or salad) works well for me since I won't get tired afterward but have the energy for the day
- Rather than having one big meal I add nuts and apples in between when I get hungry
- I also learned that I need to catch myself and have a snack before I get really hungry or I will lose all self–control (sad but true, I'm a weak person)
- I reduced milk as it gave me a slimy feeling, although I loved my latte – no more lattes
- I plan to minimize vinegar and spices as I noticed that I get heartburn from it (still working on that habit change)
- I like to go with the Chinese recommendation to follow seasons; in the winter I have more warm soups, in the summer I have more cold salads

- Learn to listen to your body instead of listening to other people's advice (including mine)! Only you can indeed find out what's right for you.

There is no one size fits all; there is only what works for you. Take ownership of your nutrition.

A LITTLE EXCURSION AND FOOD FOR THOUGHT

In TCM (Traditional Chinese Medicine), there are two sources of energy: the one that you are given at birth (prenatal) and the one that you get from nutrition (postnatal). If your energy source from food is not right, you will draw from your prenatal energy and that depot depletes without a way to refill it (prenatal energy cannot be replenished according to TCM).

Don't risk your precious prenatal energy, have good food. Go for home-made instead of produced and know what's going into your diet.

"Eat food. Not too much. Mostly plants."
Michael Pollan, In Defense of Food

WEEK 8:
SKIP SECONDS

Today's food is tasty and more abundant in calories than it ever was. We want to eat it because it tastes great and we take calories much faster than our body can notice and signal by feeling full. As a result, all western societies have a significant health problem with obesity today.

The equation for not gaining weight is dead simple. If calorie intake exceeds calories burned, you will build up fat. That's it. Nothing fancier going on. Of course, there are medical conditions that I'm excluding here, but for the majority of the population, my statement holds.

The problem is not that we want to overeat and under–exercise. The challenge is that, if left alone, we will overeat before we even notice. The meal is soooo good; we want to eat more still since we don't feel full and take another serving. Half an hour later, we feel tired, full, bloated, and look back and scratch our heads why we chose that last serving.

Modern food is rich in calories, and our caveman systems are not used to such concentration, and efficient absorption and hence don't catch it quick enough to signal our brains that we're good now. The brain still tries to get more energy in and asks for seconds (plus your caveman brain never knows when you will get food the next time).

Make a plan ahead. Skip the seconds.

There is a simple solution for this: make a plan BEFORE you start eating.

Take a decent and reasonable portion the first time. I cannot tell you how much that is; it depends on your activity level. There is much guidance available, though in books, the internet, or from people who are smarter than I am.

Once you have filled your plate with your initial portion, stick to it. Enjoy your first serving and then stop. Marvel in the aftertaste in your mouth, your teeth don't need to keep chewing to enjoy it.

If it turns out that the serving was not enough (unlikely), you will get hungry after an hour and can always eat an apple to fill the gap.

WEEK 9:
WATCH YOUR POSTURE

O ne of the lessons I learned from my teacher in martial arts many years ago (let's skip how many years ago that was to preserve my dignity and youthful image) is that your inside reflects on your outside and your outside reflects on your inside.

The critical point here is that it goes both ways.

> Your mind reflects on your body.
> Your body reflects on your mind.

When you have a great day and feel positive and strong it will show in how you stand, walk, and smile. If you have a sluggish day, are frustrated or devoid of motivation, people will be able to tell and will react to you accordingly.

However, how you present yourself and how you hold your body and posture also directly and immediately impacts how you feel. Stand upright, and you will feel more confident. Smile, and you will feel more positive. Straighten your spine, pull your shoulder blades back and open your chest and you will feel ready and open for the challenges of the day.

The beauty is that it is straightforward to control our body and posture. Everyone can smile. Everyone can straighten their posture up. It's much easier and directly controllable than telling yourself 'to be happy' or to 'feel positive'. The result is the same, and the effect is immediate.

If you don't trust my martial arts teacher, you can also check in with Harvard researcher Amy Cuddy and her famous TED Talk or book (Presence: Bringing Your Boldest Self to Your Biggest Challenges, Amy Cuddy). I like the science behind it, but at the same time, I'm always fascinated by how those old martial arts guys knew all those answers all along and way before modern science rediscovered them.

WEEK 10:
STAND MORE AT WORK

S itting all day is a main health issue these days. Our bodies were not built for sitting in the same place 10 hours per day, yet that's what most of us do. Every day. Countless studies call out the var-ious health risks re-sulting from such a sedentary life.

Break those sitting streaks!

Get a standing desk. Stand up for meetings. Drink your water, coffee, or tea standing in the kitchen, chatting with a co-worker or just looking out the window and having a moment for yourself.

To get more standing hours into your day, it's most effective to get a standing desk. If you cannot do that, take your laptop and find a place where you can stand and work for repeated times throughout your day.

However, standing all day is not great for your health either as recent studies have shown (every medicine becomes a poison if overdosed). So mix up your days with standing activities and sitting activities. Stand while working for a while, then go back to sitting and switch it back again after an hour. A mix of desk work and meetings throughout the day lends itself to that pattern.

> Switch between standing work and sitting work throughout the day. Make your default setting a standing setup to keep up with the habit.

My last tip: if you have one of those fancy standing desks that you can roll up and down, it's easy to fall back into sitting after a short, honeymoon period. It's just so comfy and relaxed. Remind yourself to get back into standing by rolling up your table to the standing position every time you leave it. That way your default, when you come back, will be to stand.

WEEK 11:
WALK AT WORK, TAKE THE LONG WAY

W e talked about standing last week and how important it is to switch between sitting and standing work. Standing is a notable improvement over sitting, but we can do better. Easily.

Get in some walking time. Take the longer route.

Our modern lives are structured around convenience, or might I say laziness. We don't need to take the stairs but can just hop into the elevator to get to the next floor. We don't need to walk to our coworker around the corner but can just message them. We don't even have to walk to meetings in the  same building anymore since we can just join virtually from our desks.

Break that laziness and get in some activity for your body throughout the day. Instead of messaging, walk. Instead of dialing into the meeting, go there. The meeting is in a different building, even better, you get more walking time. Instead of taking the elevator, walk a couple of flights of stairs. If you walk to a meeting, take the longer route, not the short cut.

Maybe now and then you can even convince your coworker to go on a walking meeting with you. Unless you need to review material in your meeting those are magic. Try it for your next 1:1.

Small changes add up, compound over time and matter a LOT in the long run. Find the ways in your daily routine in which you can squeeze in some extra movement!

WEEK 12:
GO TO THE GYM

We started with daily push-ups in week 2 and freed some extra time in the morning by skipping procrastinations in week 3.

How about we put that time to use by going to the gym in the morning at least a couple of times a week. Don't decide at the moment though, plan ahead of time what those days will be and block the time in your calendar. Get your  gym bag ready to grab the evening before.

> Make an appointment for your health. Go to the gym in the morning.

It doesn't matter whether you go for strength, cardio, or flexibility. Weights, running, or Yoga are all good. Of course, it's best if you cycle through all of them and create a balanced portfolio of workouts. You can get to that over time, though, starting with one type of exercise and then adding more variety as you advance.

However, the most important thing is that you block some real time for yourself and your health. Make an appointment with yourself to go to the gym, individually or by joining a class. See what works best for you, but make your health a priority.

WEEK 13:
END YOUR DAY WITH A MINDFULNESS EXERCISE

These days, almost every day is stressful. We are stressed at work, with our kids, our bills, you name it. Moreover, worst, it doesn't stop anymore. We're always connected, we take work home and feel guilty if we're not available 24/7.

As a result, we cannot turn off our minds and worries at night. We subsequently don't sleep well, don't get enough rest and are starting the next day on the wrong foot and even more tired. Moreover, the spiral goes further down.

> Wind down at night. Do a mindfulness exercise. Meditate, do Yoga or Tai Chi. Have pleasant dinner conversations with loved ones. Leave it there.

Break that spiral by consciously winding down at night. Specifically, try to do a mindfulness exercise at night before going to bed.

Do some meditation before you go to sleep. There are plenty of phone and Alexa apps that will guide you if you don't have experience meditating. Pick your favorite.

If meditation is not your cup of tea, do some Yoga, practice Tai Chi, stretch gently, take a bath with some candles, snuggle with your dog (or cat) or have a relaxed dinner table conversation with loved ones.

Be grateful for the day. Be grateful for friends and families. Be grateful for the experiences of the day and the ones that still lay ahead for the days coming. Great ones, and challenging ones, experiences are what makes our lives exciting and worthwhile.

Pick whatever works for you and do it. When you're home, be home. Wind down, be mindful.

Moreover, most important: don't go back to your work after a mindful break and before you sleep. Close your day and keep it closed. You don't want to stay awake all night and think about the things that 'keep you awake', you want to be relaxed and marvel about the connections and experiences you had.

WEEK 14:
BUILD AND ESTABLISH GOOD HABITS

We are now 14 weeks into building healthier habits for a more productive and balanced life. That means somewhere between 5 to 10 new habit changes already, depending on which ones and how many you decided to pick up.

Before we move on to a whole new area (being more efficient at your work), let's talk a little bit about how we make all those habits stick.

HOW DO WE MAKE THEM STICK?

How can we avoid to flip–flop from new habit to a new habit every week and bouncing back to bad behaviors as soon as we take our eyes off a recent habit change?

In the past, I've tried to follow the rule that you have to keep a habit for 30 days to make it stick, but to be honest more often than not this didn't work for me. More recently, I came across two books that provide useful frameworks that do work (at least for me).

- **"Mini Habits", Stephen Guise** – A simple to read book that focuses on making habits so small, that you cannot possibly fail to just do them.
- **"Atomic Habits", James Clear** – A more scientific exploration of the topic with many suggestions on how to make habits stick.

The following is a summary of the rules I found most useful from those books. Read the books for more suggestions as well as the science behind them.

ONE SMALL CHANGE AT A TIME

Don't boil the ocean! You will get frustrated and will give up.

Don't try to change more than one behavior or add more than one habit at a time. Don't pick habits that reflect your end goal, but rather focus on the next immediate step that will get you there.

> Don't boil the ocean. Pick one habit at a time.
> Make your habit changes too small to fail.

Instead, pick one habit per week and focus on it. Focus on only that habit until you reliably repeat it. Then you can add a new habit to your list. If you notice that you stopped doing the previous change, go back and add that habit back again.

Make your habit change small. Instead of trying to turn end goals into a habit, focus on the immediate next step. For example, instead of saying "I will lose 10 pounds", make it a habit to drink a refreshing glass of water every time you want to grab your habitual can of soda.

Make your habit changes small; make them easy. Make them too small to fail.

Small changes add up. Rather than making a heroic effort and keeping it for two weeks, make incremental 1% changes and keep going at them for the rest of your life. Nothing beats the impact of consistency (the "Compounding effect of 1% changes.", James Clear).

DON'T BREAK YOUR STREAK

Once a new habit is indeed a habit, you will do it naturally. Until then, you need to 'manage' yourself to stick to it. Usually, the best way to do that is to track and keep a log that holds you accountable.

> Track your progress to keep you going. Don't break your streak. Never fail twice.

Tracking your progress helps to keep you motivated as you see the rewarding days, when you kept with your habit, adding up. It also serves to hold you accountable because once you have a chain of successful days, you don't want to break the streak.

How you track your habit doesn't matter as long as you do it. Find the way that works best for you: a wall calendar that you tick off, your journal, a jar of marbles that you fill up every time you did a specific habit, an app on your phone that you always have with you. I like to use both a wall calendar for a big longterm habit that I'm chasing, as well as an iPhone app (Streaks) to keep track of my progress on the small changes throughout the day.

Try your best not to break a streak. It is motivational to see how you add day after day to your list of little wins. Try not to drop the ball; work hard not to break the streak.

Having that said, life will happen. Now and then something will come in the way of your habit. That is a crucial point in your habit–forming. One of two things will happen: 1) you broke your streak and will now have a much lower bar to dropping the habit again the next day or 2) you get right back to your habit the next day. To be honest, the first response is much more likely, and it dooms you for failure on your desired long-term changes. The most significant risk to a habit is not the start but keeping to go.

To prevent you from dropping your habit once you face the first obstacle, make it a point to never fail twice in a row. It's ok to fail every now and again. However, NEVER fail twice in a row to exercise your habit.

As a side note for habit tracking apps: I like the iOS Streak app, which lets me track six habits at a time. If I successfully did a habit for six weeks, it most likely sticks, and I can replace it with a new one. If it doesn't hold yet, I will wait a little longer before I take on the next habit. Tracking six habits at a time is a reasonable balance between ambition and feasibility.

MAKE IT AUTOMATIC

Your will power drains through the day. Have a plan. Make your habits a reflex.

We all start our days with the best intentions. We stick to our priorities through the morning, and then the curveballs start hitting us. We get tired; we get worn out. We come home exhausted, drop in front of the TV, have a couple of drinks. Then we go to bed, slightly frustrated about ourselves and have the best intentions to be more disciplined the next day. The next day won't be any different, though.

> Have a plan. Make good habits easy and bad habits difficult. Make your habit a reflex. Identify trigger points.

The problem is that we cannot trust ourselves as we get more and more tired throughout the day, and our willpower gets depleted by the obstacles, challenges, and decisions we are facing.

We need our fresh mind to make the right decisions for us. We need your well-rested brain, with its full reservoir of will power and sight of the right priorities to make the decisions for us, before the tired brain can kick in and take over.

Make a proactive plan of 'if, then' decisions. You will be tired in the evening when you come home. Make a plan what you will do when you want to drop in front of the TV ("when I want to grab the TV remote, I will rather pick up a cup of tea and the book I started reading"). Make the plan while you still have your priorities straight, not when you're tired. That way, you will not need to decide when you're tired, you will only need to execute.

Identifying and setting triggers for your habits is an additional technique that you can use. Put your gym bag in front of your door so that you have to pick it up on your way to work. Make fruit and veggies visibly available in your house and make candy hard to reach. Put away the remote and place a book in its place. Get the TV out of your bedroom, set nighttime timers that switch off your devices and lights.

You can also add a new habit to something that you already do habitually ("when I grab my morning coffee, I will do ten push-ups"). It's an easy way to trigger a new good behavior through behavior that is already ingrained in your daily life.

Make your habit a reflex, so you no longer need to make a conscious decision. Make good habits easy and bad habits challenging to start.

WORK BACKWARDS FROM WHO YOU WANT TO BE

> "Identity is stronger than goals. Your believes of yourself drive your behavior."
> James Clear, Atomic Habits

So far, we talked about how you can make particular behaviors stick. It's a very narrow approach and requires will power. After all, you want to change something AGAINST what you perceive as your natural preferences.

To take this to the next level, you need to change your natural preferences. You need to change who you think you are and what preferences that person has. You need to change your image of yourself.

> Decide what type of person you are and then make the decisions such a person would make.

However, don't get stuck at dreaming about what type of person you would wish to be. Decide what type of person you are.

Are you a healthy person? Are you a person who doesn't drink alcohol? Are you a person that exercises every day? Are you a person that spends quality time with his kids and family every day? Are you a person that creates a piece of art every day? Are you a person who helps someone every day?

Decide who you ARE. Then make the decisions such a person will make.

Are you a person who doesn't drink alcohol? Well, then it's easy, you don't need to buy beer anymore, and you don't need to mull over whether you should have a drink at the work party or not. You're a person that doesn't drink alcohol. Period.

Many years ago I decided that I never want to drive after having had a drink anymore (I never had an accident or issue up to then, but I also didn't want to take the risk anymore). I didn't know back then, but I decided not to be a person who drives after they had a drink. I never once did since then, nor did I miss it.

For in the moment decisions, it doesn't matter as much what longterm goals you have or what person you would wish to become when you grow up. What matters is what person you decided that you are already and what decisions such a person makes.

Decide what person you are TODAY and make the decisions such a person would make.

PART II
BE MORE EFFECTIVE

Don't waste your time. Get the most out of it.

WEEK 15:
DON'T WASTE YOUR COMMUTE

We spend many hours every week at work. For most office workers it's 40–60 hours. Side note: folks who tell you they work more are most likely just showing off, or they add a lot of inefficient time to their workdays. That is a massive chunk of our lives. We better make it count!

Step one is to make your commute count. I don't know for you, but for me, that's another 2–3 hours on top of my work day. Every day.

> Make your commute count. Triage your email, get on top of your calendar. Listen to a good audiobook or NPR. Call your parents at least once a week.

If you ride your bike to work, you can skip ahead to the next tip. You already make your commute count – you do something good for your health.

Kudos if you use the train and bus and board it early enough to secure a seat. Instead of checking Facebook, get your laptop, and do some email triage. That takes time but usually doesn't require too much deep focus.

You might as well get it done before you even enter the office. Sort your calendar; get ahead of things. Know what's coming and be aware of the fires that await you as soon as you approach your desk.

If you need to drive yourself (like I do), listen to a good audiobook. Learn something new while your mind is still fresh, empty, and ready to take something in, instead of being distracted by a hundred things shouting for your attention. Don't listen to the local radio station or the comedy show. Check out NPR podcasts or pick a good audiobook.

If you don't want to listen to a book, call your parents. They will appreciate it, and years down the road you will be glad you did take the time to call them. Make it a point to do this at least once a week. Call them while you commute, so you don't have any excuse not to do it.

WEEK 16:
TAKE CONTROL OF YOUR PRIORITIES

There are many things that we should or could do. All of them will keep us busy. Few of them will have a lasting impact and move us forward.

Focus on the things that matter! Prioritize what needs to get done. Plan your priorities and block time for them.

Write down YOUR priorities and what YOU need to achieve. Write it down and make a purposeful commitment to yourself. Revisit and update that list every day. It's an excellent preparation for the day while you sip your morning coffee.

Pick the 3 to 4 things that you want to achieve in the week and the 1 or 2 things that you will get down for the day. Don't pick more; focus on what needs to get done this week and today. Be realistic as to what you actually can get done, given the unplanned distractions that will pull on your attention and time as the day progresses.

As you write down your priorities, make sure to follow these four rules:

BE SPECIFIC

Don't write down 'get more organized', be specific and write down 'compile a list of the things I need to fix in my backyard'.

MAKE IT ACHIEVABLE

Don't write down 'declutter the house'. It will probably take a while to achieve that end goal. Be specific about the step you want to accomplish today or this week, for example, 'clean up the kitchen'.

BLOCK TIME

If you don't block time on your calendar, other supposedly urgent things will come along and distract you. With that, your priorities will only be good intentions, and when you look back at the end of the week, you will be utterly frustrated. Defend that blocked time against other 'important' things that try to push over it.

DON'T FORGET TO ADD TIME FOR YOUR VALUES

With all the things we HAVE to do, we often forget to take time for the things we WANT to do. Block time for the things that are important to you and that help you live to your values. Add them to your weekly and daily priorities. They are just as much, if not more important than everything else.

WEEK 17:
WHAT'S ON YOUR WORRY LIST?

We all have a to-do list (I assume), but do you also have a worry-list?

We are usually pretty good at tracking the things we

need to do, but we often miss paying attention to risks. Those risks tend to turn into issues at the worst moment and often prevent us from achieving a goal (or at least require last-minute firefights).

Think about all the things that could go wrong. What are you worried about? Then find solutions or mitigations for each and burn down that list to zero.

It's a good practice to start a worry-list when you start a new project. Probably even before you begin a to-do list.

GET A HANDLE ON ALL THINGS THAT COULD GO WRONG

Start listing the things that could go wrong. Look at that list from all different angles (e.g., resourcing changes, stakeholder alignment, changing assumptions, ambiguity on details and data) to make it as comprehensive as possible.

Keep adding to that list as you go deeper into the project, learn more, and discover new risks and challenges. Think about all the possible worst–case scenarios and what they would mean for your goal (Special Forces teams do a similar scenario-play exercise before going into a mission).

Your worry list should contain:

- Big risks for your goal
- Upcoming or anticipated challenges
- Big open questions and any areas of ambiguity

GET ON A GLIDE PATH TO BLISS

Once you have your list, make it a point and recurring check to burn down that list. Treat it like a bug list – burn down issue by issue and make sure you have a glide path to zero way before your project is due.

Be clear and understand which items on your worry list need to be resolved first, and by what time. What needs to come next? What project steps do need which issues to be addressed? What are the long poles that take more time to figure out?

Track risks carefully so that you will spot early if a risk turns into a real issue (dependencies to other people or teams are an excellent example for this).

If you don't have one, start a worry list for your key priorities today.

WEEK 18:
DECLARE WAR ON PROCRASTINATION AND WASTED TIME

Did you check Facebook, Instagram or LinkedIn updates today? Did you play a game on your phone? For how long? Did you wonder where the time went? Did you feel better and more satisfied afterward, or did it leave a little sour taste in your mouth?

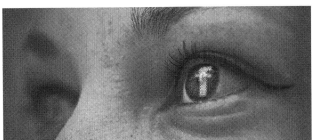

Don't get me wrong; it's ok to use social media and play games. As long as you do it deliberately. In martial arts, we learn that the key to everything is to make conscious decisions, take deliberate action, and be aware of what's going on.

> Make conscious decisions, take deliberate action, and be aware of the time you spend.

If you feel like playing a game, do so for all means. However, decide before, how long you want to play and be deliberate as to what else you will not do to play that game. Make a conscious decision to not go in the yard to smell flowers because you want to play that game for 30 mins.

Do not just do those things so that you don't have to tackle a chore you didn't want to do.

Years ago, Uli and I would watch TV in the evenings. We would sit down, hop across channels, watch shows that we only halfway liked and endured commercials. Since we rarely found something that was genuinely satisfying, we kept looking for much of the evening and went to bed way too late, only to be groggy and cranky the next morning. We don't have cable anymore. On weekends we often watch one movie with our kids (one for the weekend) and have much fun doing so. Otherwise, the screen stays off.

Same for social media. A few years ago, I used to spend much time on Facebook feeds or news outlets (the real ones, not all the made–up fake news). I hardly ever got satisfied, and I rarely felt better. Now I get up in the morning, take a shower and go to work right away. As a result, I come home to my kids a little earlier in the evening. I don't miss anything but gain a lot. I do check Facebook on Saturday mornings, but I do it deliberately (I might even stop that since the news feed gets worse every time).

Decide how you want to spend your time. Set a limit. Track the limit. Don't just do it to have an excuse to be lazy. If you're going to be lazy, make it deliberately and proudly.

In the beginning, it can help to set yourself screen time limits. Monitor how you do spend time and decide what it should be. Write it down. Then start controlling your time. Turn off the screen. Cancel your cable subscription.

Only do what gives you real longterm pleasure – it's likely not your screen.

However, please do get me right. If you love Facebook, a game, a TV show and get pleasure and satisfaction from it every time you watch it, please do so. Likewise, procrastination doesn't only come in the form of digital media. You might as well procrastinate fiddling around in the house because you don't want to get yourself to the office work. Doing dishes has so much more appeal during tax season than in the months after you turned in your taxes.

> Control your procrastinations. Do them deliber-
> ately (or not at all).

WEEK 19:
TAKE TIME MANAGEMENT TO THE NEXT LEVEL

D o you know how you spend your time through the week? Do you really know? If I would ask you, could you tell me how much of your time you have spent on each of the different topics you care about?

Most people have a general guesstimate but don't know for sure. Most people are also dead wrong with their guesses.

If you don't track your time, you cannot manage it.

"You can't manage what you can't measure."
Peter Drucker

If you want to become more proactive and deliberate with how you spend your time and attention, you need to be intentional about it. You need to decide what your time should be spent on, measure how you actually spend time and then take corrective action if those two measures don't align.

Decide how you should spend your time. Track how you spend it. Adjust where needed. Rinse and repeat.

It's fairly easy to be more intentional about our time:

MAKE A PLAN

The first step to more intentional time control is to decide how you should spend your time. What are the different categories that you care about, and what percentage of time should you spend on each? For example, some of my categories are 'people management', 'planning', 'execution', 'hiring', and so on.

MEASURE YOUR ACTUAL TIME ALLOCATION

Once you have a plan, you need to gather data. Measure how you spend your time. You can do this in a dedicated time log or use categories in a calendar that you already use. It requires almost zero effort to categorize meetings that are already on your schedule. Same for times that you had previously blocked to focus on your priorities. Now all you need to do is to fill in the time in between, for example when you caught up on email. I would guess for a typical knowledge worker 80% of your time is already on your calendar anyway. Take an inventory for everything, including the times when you procrastinate. Otherwise, your time log is useless.

DON'T STOP AT MEASURING

Block time for the things that are important for you. When you see that the times that are scheduled by others run out of boundaries, block some work time off before others block the time for you.

CHECK DAILY AND ADJUST AS YOU GO

Do a quick visual check every day. Look more thoroughly back and forward once a week. Adjust as you need it. If you use color coding for your categories, it will be easy to get a good sense with just a glance.

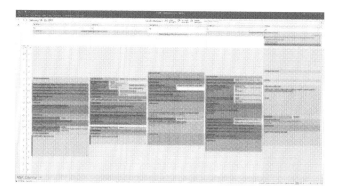

REPORT OUT AND HOLD YOURSELF ACCOUNTABLE

Once a month, run a report. If you use Outlook, all you need to do is to export your calendar into a CSV file and then copy the data into Excel. Below is a link to a template that you can use to run some reports and graphical analysis on your raw data. Track your time allocation over time. Are you trending in the right direction?

https://keruumabudo.files.wordpress.com/2019/02/time-allocation-template.xlsx

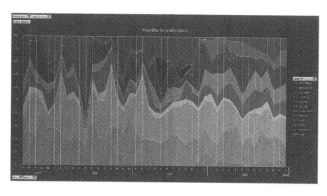

UPDATE YOUR CATEGORIES

Don't be stuck with the categories you picked a while ago. Adjust what you track as your priorities change. Update your categories as you want to drive new and different behaviors. You should do this at least once a quarter. For example, I recently added the category 'deep work' when I realized that I got drawn into too many tactical directions.

Here are some pointers that can help you find the right categories:

- Your job description
- What you need to improve and your growth opportunities
- What you are passionate about
- How your mentors or role models think about their time

Time management is fun! It takes only little energy if you align it with the tools you already use, and it will teach you a lot about how you spend your days and energy.

The key is to pick categories that make sense for the outcomes that you want to achieve. Pick categories that will teach you interesting insights about your days and your subconscious preferences. My categories won't work for you; you need to find your own!

WEEK 20:
START TIME BOXING

Work and time have that funny relationship, where a given task always takes exactly as much time as you have allocated for it.

If you have planned an hour to catch up on your email, it will take an hour. If you have planned 30 mins, then you most likely will get just as much done. If you give yourself an afternoon to clean the yard, it will take an afternoon. If you give yourself  the whole weekend, it will surely take that long (and you likely won't even get finished).

Even worse, if you don't set a time limit, chances are that you will keep on working (or being distracted), without ever getting the job done.

> Set yourself an aggressive time limit and then get the job done in that time.

If you set yourself an aggressive time limit to get a job done, you box it into a specific space in your calendar — you time box.

Timeboxing (if you took an aggressive time frame) will make you prioritize. It will help you focus on getting the job done and prevent you from getting distracted because you feel you have all the time in the world. You're on a clock; you have to be efficient. Because you have to be efficient you will be efficient.

Also, plan a little break time after your time box. Focus and push but know that you will be able to let go and relax a little afterward.

Find what timeframes work for you. Few people get a meaningful amount of things done in periods shorter than 30 mins. It just takes a while to get mentally organized and started. Likewise, our concentration tends to go down after hours, and it is usually a good idea to take a break.

Notice when you can no longer keep up the concentration and take a break. When I feel that I get inefficient in the evening, I will go home. There might be work left, but I will be more effective and efficient the next morning. At that stage, an hour sleep is worth more than an hour pretend–work.

WEEK 21:
SAY 'NO' THE RIGHT WAY

We all have lots on our plates. By design, we have more things we could do than what we can actually deliver in the given time.

That forces us to make prioritizations and double down on the most impactful things.

With that, it's essential to know how to say 'no.' Here is how I say 'no' if I need to. Moreover, how I appreciate others saying 'no' so that I can manage around it.

SAYING 'NO' THE RIGHT WAY

It's ok to say 'no.' In fact, people expect you to be honest enough to say 'no' if you will not be able to do something.

It's not ok to say 'yes,' but then fail to follow through on your promises or to raise the flag the last-minute.

> Say 'no' early. Help people understand why you need to say 'no.' Offer alternatives. Escalate quickly if plans change.

So how do you say 'no' the right way?

START WITH THE 'WHY' (AS ALWAYS)

Explain why you cannot do something. Explain what else you need to do during the same time and why you think that is more important. Provide the background so that others can follow your decision.

If you need to say 'no' to your boss, explain to her how you are prioritizing and why you think another task is more important. If she doesn't agree, list the things that are competing for your time. Ask which one you should drop instead.

Don't just take on an additional task, hoping you will be able to deliver it without knowing when you would do that feat. Most people prefer an honest push–back over a best of intentions but unrealistic commitment that won't be followed through.

UNDERSTAND TIMELINES

Not everything needs to happen right now. In fact, very few things are truly urgent, although many are perceived or presented as urgent.

Ask for when a task is due. Check your calendar and priorities and see when you can fit it in. Offer that plan and check for agreement.

Be realistic and ask people for true timelines. Many people will buffer when they really need something. Ask them to give you the real deadline, but then also make sure that you will be ready by that time. Otherwise, you just teach them to add additional buffers in the future.

OFFER ALTERNATIVES

Try to find alternatives if priorities and timelines don't line up. Maybe you cannot do the update this week because you need to work on an important paper for the team, but your coworker can take the work off your shoulder this time? Maybe the project update this week is not as urgent as it appears and it will be covered anyway in your more thorough update that is coming two weeks from now. Maybe the offsite follow–up can wait a week since you have already blocked some dedicated follow–up time next week.

Understand the true urgency and then plan for it. Find alternatives if things don't fit but need to get done. For whatever plan, timeline or alternatives you offer – make sure you actually plan and block time for it!

ESCALATE EARLY IF PLANS CHANGE

Only one thing is worse for a manager than a team member who comes the day before a deadline to tell you that he won't get the work done in time: a team member who tells you the day off.

As soon as you realize that plans won't happen as initially scheduled, you need to let everyone who counts on your deliverable know. Give a heads–up as early as possible. Have checkpoints ahead of your deadline so that you will know right away if things get out of control.

Escalate early! Given enough time to react, there is almost always another solution. If you only learn about an issue the last–minute, there is usually little that can be done.

Similarly, if you need to de-prioritize or altogether drop work that you had initially planned, you need to let everyone who is waiting on you know as quickly as possible.

Again, the 'why' does the trick. Explain why things needed to change, what you had to prioritize. If possible at all, offer a new timeline or another solution. Check if that's ok for the person who was counting on you. Don't just drop the bomb, or even worse, don't let the other person find out on their own.

WEEK 22:
PACE YOURSELF

If we want to grow, we need to push ourselves. We need to go beyond our comfort zone and do what's hard. To build a muscle, we need to stress it to the point where is tires out. The same is true for other areas in which we learn and grow.

However, and this is critically important, we also need to slow down and recover. Our abilities grow when we slow down after a stretch push. Our muscles grow in the recovery times, to get ready for the next time when we stress them more than usual.

> Pace yourself. Decide when to push hard and
> when to slow down and recover. Recover and
> grow. Get ready for the next time you will need to
> push.

Without those downtimes and recovery periods, we won't get better. Our muscles will not grow. Likewise, our abilities will not grow if we operate always and exclusively at the point where we're close to breaking.

We grow from pushing, speeding up, and then consciously slowing down and relaxing again.

We grow if we stretch ourselves, but ONLY if we also allow our muscles and mind to regenerate. Otherwise, we just burn out. Pace yourself!

As you take on stretch assignments or go hard to meet an important deadline, make it a point to also plan in (and take) the following recovery time. For me, it's weekdays versus weekends. Find out what it is for you.

When you take a recovery time, do it fully. Athletes don't practice during their recovery period. You shouldn't either. Stay away from work, emails, and texts during that time. Come back afterward, refreshed and stronger.

WEEK 23:
DON'T GET STUCK IN END–GOAL OBSESSION

We are all too often focused (fixated) on the end goal and forget about the necessary individual steps that lead us there. Since we don't know precisely how to reach our goals, we don't make progress and get increasingly frustrated.

The problem is that most individuals, leaders, and businesses focus on output metrics and try to improve them. At Amazon, I've learned to focus on improving input metrics instead. It's a powerful shift in mindset if you want to have real impact.

> Focus on the things you can manage. Measure inputs and real-time metrics rather than outputs. Design your metrics to support your long-term plan, not short–term gains.

THE PROBLEM WITH OUTPUT METRICS

Output metrics (e.g., profit, user base, user retention, downloads) are the outcomes that a business wants to achieve, and the ultimate goal is to improve them as much as possible.

The only issue with that is that output metrics or business outcomes are the results of many right or wrong actions that have already been taken and many right or wrong decisions that have already been made in the past. It's very hard to look at a lagging profit or user metric and figure out what to do specifically. Moreover, by the time the output metric is lagging, it's in most cases also too late to course correct anyway.

INPUT METRICS HELP SHAPE OUTCOMES

The better metrics to look at are input metrics. Input metrics are measurements of the things that need to go right to generate excellent outcomes. At Amazon, we focus on input metrics first and foremost.

For example, if you build a new app and want to grow your user base quickly and sustainably, you should not spend all your energy looking at the number of users. Probably you shouldn't look at that at all for the first few months. Instead, you need to get your inputs in shape. For instance, is your product what users want (what's your app's rating in the store, what are the negative feedbacks from users)? Are your marketing campaigns effective (what are click-through rates, how is your conversion rate for downloads and sign-ups)?

Focus on inputs more than on the outputs when you look at the funnel. Input metrics are early warnings. They are also much more actionable than output metrics. It's much easier to react on leading click-through rates or customer feedback about insufficient UX than to look at low usage numbers and guess what might be wrong.

FOCUSING ON INPUTS SETS YOU UP FOR THE LONG RUN

Too much focus on output metrics can also incentivize you to make bad long–term decisions to gain short–term benefits (just look at Wall Street to get an abundance of examples). Focusing on input metrics will guide you to build the right systems and set the right priorities for long–term growth.

I saw an example of that conflict just recently during MBA interviews. I asked candidates how they would decide which of two prices (same product, different suppliers, different pricing) they would offer to a customer. Most candidates will provide the standard answer: "the price that offers the best margin and thus the best profit for the company as long as it's within the constraints (buying power) of the customer." That answer maximizes the output metric (profit).

If you focus on input metrics, the above is the wrong answer (and btw, don't give that answer in an Amazon interview). Your input metric is to have lots of happy returning customers who trust you. If customers are happy, return often, and trust you, they will do great business with you over time. The right answer is to "always offer the best price to the customer." It's the better long–term strategy, and it will drive the right outcomes. That's why at Amazon customer obsession always comes first.

CLOSING WITH A NON–BUSINESS EXAMPLE

To drive home the point, I want to close with a non–business example.

As you know by now, I care a lot about living a healthy life. Moreover, I believe in measuring progress.

In the past, I did track my progress on outcomes like my weight, my overall fitness (how do you even define that?) my energy levels, and so on. You get the idea. The problem is that those 'metrics' change slowly and are pretty hard to influence directly since they are the result of many things playing together.

In recent years I changed my focus to a small set of input metrics: (1) exercise every single day, (2) sleep 8 hours a day and (3) drink 2 liters of water every day. Those metrics are simple, they are accurate on a daily basis, and I know exactly what to do if I miss any of them. They are also straightforward to track on my Fitbit or Apple watch.

You might guess it already, but since having that focus, I saw significant improvements on my fitness, weight, energy, and a general feeling of wellbeing without actually focusing on any of those outcome metrics specifically.

WEEK 24:
REMOVE DISTRACTIONS

Do you envy the artist who is immersed in his painting or the monk who seems to be lost in his meditation? The trick to get there is to tune out all distractions. If we do something that we truly and deeply love, this can happen by itself. For example, as you get fully immersed when you watch your favorite team playing.

However, more often than not, we get distracted by something shiny and exciting popping up just when we started to get into our task. It takes up to 20 mins to fully get back into a task once distracted.

> Remove all distractions. Observe what catches your attention and turn it off until you decide to take a break. Deliberately switch between deep focus and unfocused catch–up.

Unless you want to challenge your inner monk and develop focus despite external distractions, you should make your life easier by just eliminating them.

TURN OFF NOTIFICATIONS

A classic distractor is any notifications on your computer or phone. Beeping sounds and popping windows for emails, text messages, IMs or even stupid system notifications pop in our visual field all the time (and the beeping makes sure, we notice even if we don't look at our phone).

Turn off all notifications. I mean, all of them. On my computer and phone, I have no email or text notifications. The only thing that I allow to interrupt me is a text from my wife or kids. Anything else can wait.

Put your phone on silent while you work, or better even, turn it off. If a call was important, the caller would leave a message. Personally, I never answer the phone, but that's a different story and probably a little too nerdy for most.

When you have break time, go back to your email, pick up your phone, and check if there is something important that requires your attention.

Work in spurts – spurts of deep attention, and then spurts of catching up with distractions.

SNOOZE MESSAGES

You can even snooze emails or text messages for a period of time when you don't want to be distracted. It's easy to create rules for that in your email client, and your phone can be put into airplane mode.

Turn your email and texts off for the weekend. I have a rule in my Outlook client that directs my work email to a folder that I won't see on my phone on the weekend. That rule lets through messages that are marked as urgent. Everything else has to wait until Monday.

FOCUS ON ONE APP AT A TIME

Now that we have turned off interrupting notifications, we will take it one step further. Kill multitasking.

Windows on a computer look nice. Moreover, they distract, dividing your focus across multiple apps.

Do one task at a time. Don't allow distractions in your peripheral vision. Close all windows but the one you are working on. If you don't want to do that, open the window/application you're working in full–screen.

Modern computers support multiple virtual desktops. Move your focus app to a clean desktop where nothing else is opened. Ban the distractions in your peripheral vision.

Focus on what you do. One thing at a time.

Deliberately change between one app and checking multiple inputs and signals. Make a choice whether you are tactical or strategic. Both are important but not at the same time.

WEEK 25:
INBOX ZERO, REGAIN CONTROL OF YOUR INBOX

Almost everyone I talk to is struggling with email overload. Interesting enough, that is regardless of whether they receive ten emails a day or 100. In my different roles, I have typically received about 100 emails a day, not counting discussion groups, newsletters, advertising, or spam (which all  get filtered out automatically before they reach my inbox).

I always make it a point to have my inbox down to 1–2 screens at the end of the day and to Zero on Friday by the time I leave the office.

'Inbox zero' is my golden rule for the weekend. Moreover, while it sounds like a tough challenge, it's actually very achievable. Decades of working at Microsoft and Amazon, with email as the primary tool of communication, have taught me how to do this.

BAD NEWS FIRST

As you follow the tech news, every couple of months, you will hear about a groundbreaking new tool/technology that will finally "kill email" and make communications so "much more effective."

I hate to break it to you, but that's not going to happen. The amount of information that is shared is the problem, not the tool. When you jump on a new tool, you will find some relief for a while because no one else is there yet. Of course, you get less spam and more focused communications if only you and your best buddy are on that new cool thing. Once the tool has enough audience to be usable, the volume of conversations will feel unmanageable again. A couple of examples throughout IT history are email, SMS, IM, Twitter, Facebook, WhatsApp, LinkedIn, Yammer, Slack,…

The only things that truly work are your process and discipline.

KEEP IT SIMPLE (BUT KEEP TO IT)!

The good news is that this information problem can be solved. All it requires is a plan and a little discipline.

Keep it simple and stick to it.

Finish easy stuff right away, mark things that take more time and block that time on your calendar.

Delete everything that isn't immediate relevant.

Move it to <u>one</u> archive folder if you have separation anxiety.

Don't sort messages you want to keep into many folders – search is your friend.

For me, simplicity is key. If a process is not simple, I will likely not stick to it over a longer period of time. That's why I stopped using categories and lots of folders for to-dos and elaborate filing. In most times, it would not be clear where something belongs, and I would have trouble finding it again later.

All I need is my inbox (contains everything I still have to take care of), a follow-up flag (marks things that need a little more time) and a single archive folder (to get rid of anything that is done or not relevant right now).

You don't need more than one folder to keep things that are already done. Search is awesome. Trust it! (Or get a better email system if your search doesn't work.)

Rule 1: When you touch it, triage it

When you touch an email, triage it (or even better resolve it). Don't ever go to the same email twice to decide what to do with it. Make that decision right there on the spot.

Every email that you receive typically falls into one of 4 categories:

- 20% – Can be answered or delegated in less than a minute.
- 10% – Needs more time to follow–up.
- 40% – You shouldn't have received this in the first place.
- 30% – Is informational but you might just as well live a happy life without that information.

Rule 2: Delete everything that you don't really care about

This includes old newsletters that you signed up for in a previous life, the org updates that don't even remotely relate to what you're doing, the email that you got CCed on without anyone knowing why, or the follow-up that someone else in your team is taking care of (delegation is king!).

Get those out of your inbox right away!

Tip: If you are anxious about deleting emails that you might want to get back to later, move them to your (single) archive folder. I am one of those anxious folks, and I use that workaround. I still wait for the day when I get back to any of those emails. Storage is cheap and unlimited email is the norm these days (I have a free 50GB mailbox and, as much as I try, can't get it fuller than 15%).

Rule 3: Answer quick things while you look at them

There is no value in not answering a simple email right away. You have just spent some time reading it. Do you want to spend that time again?

If it's less than a minute, answer right away. Then move that email out of your inbox into your archive folder (or delete it – depending on how adventurous you feel).

Rule 4: Block time for responses that need a deeper follow–up

Some emails require more thinking, a longer write-up, some research, or just some emotional distance because you are so enraged.

Flag them for follow–up and stop reading (you will have forgotten the details by the time you actually follow up). Move on to the next unread email that needs to get triaged.

Remember to block time on your calendar for when you will go through all flagged emails (and only those!) and get them done.

Rule 5: If you think you will read it within the week, then keep it (for now)

There are some emails that seem to be interesting enough to read in a spare moment but just not important enough or too long to read right now. (I'm guilty of sending my wife a lot of these – my official apologies for that.)

Sometimes those spare moments will come, and you will discover interesting new things. Often you won't find a spare moment, and those emails will pile up (the ones that don't have a flag and are marked as read but still linger around in your inbox).

Here's my bonus rule: If I didn't have time to read them by Friday, then they have to go forever. It's a liberating feeling to bulk–move all of them into your archive folder Friday evening.

Don't put those emails in a special folder; you will never get back to it anyway.

APPROACHING BLISS

After this triage exercise, your inbox will have shrunk dramatically. You have answered everything that was quick or urgent. You will have marked things that need more time and will know exactly what needs and what doesn't need attention.

Everything is read, and the only unread stuff is new emails that are coming in and will be triaged in your next triage session (not now!).

I try never to let that remaining list grow more than one or max two screens long. If it gets longer, delete some of the FYI emails and/or block more time for follow-ups.

For Fridays, your goal should be to have zero emails in your inbox. Then turn off your emails over the weekend and spend quality time with your family instead. Create a rule to have them moved to a separate folder so that they don't show up in your phone's inbox.

This will feel really good! Stick to it for a while and get motivated by the sense of control that you will gain.

Please make a deliberate difference between 'triage' and 'follow–up' mode. I make it a point to triage all of my emails first thing in the morning. So when I start my day of meetings, I have already minimized the number of surprises waiting for me. Moreover, I can feel confident not checking email throughout the day unless I have spare time for it.

SOME WEEKS ARE HARDER

Some weeks are harder. There are more emails coming in. You have more other things going on. You just aren't that effective.

I simply adjust my system for that, by significantly raising the bar for emails that I keep in my inbox for 'later reading.' If you send me something as FYI during an extra–busy week – tough luck for you (and my heartfelt apologies).

Even in crazy weeks, I hold true to my rules of (1) no more than two screens of emails in my inbox and (2) inbox zero on Friday afternoon.

IT'S WORTH IT

Get rid of the guilt, the lingering thoughts about your email, the anxiety that you might have missed something (or even worse the revelation that you did miss something important).

Inbox zero is a blessing! Treat yourself to it. I have an empty inbox every Friday evening, and it makes for an excellent start into the weekend!

INTENTIONAL USE OF TECHNOLOGY

Here's a little tip on how technology can help you stay focused on triaging versus answering. Moreover, it also helps with not re-reading the same email again and again

Triaging: use your mobile phone

Mobile phones are great for this. Use spare minutes to triage new emails on your phone. Make a triage decision after the first paragraph (reading on a small screen is a pain anyway) or provide a short (!) answer if possible.

Hold yourself back from reading long emails that you won't answer on the spot. You can even set your email client to only show 'unread' emails so you won't be tempted to re-read emails that you had already touched.

Answering: use your desktop/laptop

Respond to more complex emails when you have time at your desk (with a nice keyboard).

Don't triage, focus only on those emails that you have marked for follow–up. Get the list down towards zero as much as possible during that time.

Intentional separation

Separating triage time from answering time will make you more effective with both. Moreover, since my proposed systems are technology–wise super simple (all it needs is the ability to flag), it will work and transfer across any email system and client.

> Chose the best technology for the task to force you into the right habits!

WEEK 26:
BRING A LITTLE ZEN INTO YOUR LIFE

CLEAN UP YOUR WORKSPACE

L et's look at your workspace (office desk, kitchen counter, tool shed). How much stuff is lying around and cluttering your workspace, and your mind as a result?

If you want to be able to focus on your work and come up with creative ideas, you need to remove distractions. Create white spaces.

Create empty spaces. Reduce distractions.

Clean up your workspace. Find a place for everything and preferably pick a spot that you cannot see. The only things that should be on your workspace are the project that you are working on <u>right now</u> and the tools that you are using <u>right now</u>.

Everything else needs to go and find a place somewhere else. Likewise, everything needs to have its place. Moreover, it needs to be there and only there unless it's in your hands.

If everything has its place and can always be found there, you will also not need to make a mad dash through your house to find it when you need it (think: your keys). I believe the creative chaos is a myth. I trust the empty and creative Zen space instead.

> "Order is contagious."
> Roy Baumeister, John Tierney, Willpower

If your workspace is not clean and quiet, your mind won't be either.

Create your retreat space in which your brain can calm down, and your mind can focus.

CREATE EMPTY SPACE IN TIME

Don't stop at cleaning and emptying your workspace. Also, create free space in time. Free up time on your calendar, for which you plan to do nothing.

No, that's not the same as not having a concrete plan an instead running random errands. Plan out a time where you do <u>nothing</u>. Create space for your mind and observe what will happen.

It might be scary at first but try it out. Soon it will feel liberating. Give yourself the gift of time without expectations and without things you have to do or achieve.

> Give yourself the gift of a little Zen. With emptiness comes focus. With focus come results and inspiration.

Empty spaces ignite your creativity – both empty spaces in space as well as in time (do nothing times).

WEEK 27:
AVOID FIREFIGHTS

Have you heard someone say before: "I do my best work when I'm under pressure with tight timelines"? I call BS on that; it's just a sign of bad time management, poor planning and lack of discipline.

Don't wait to the last–minute. Plan ahead. Finish your tasks as soon as possible.

While waiting for the last–minute increases the pressure on you and will help you to stop procrastinating, it is also immensely stressful, especially if any additional unplanned but urgent work gets added on top.

Work under pressure is not your best work, even if you might think so because you have trained yourself over the years to only take last-minute work serious.

Rather take control. Plan out your work and try to get it done as early as possible. That allows you to do the job when you have time. It will also avoid that you might end up in a situation where two urgent tasks (one known, the other one unexpected) will have the same deadline.

Getting on tasks early increases your degrees of freedom and dramatically reduces your stress levels. All it takes is a little planning ahead and some discipline.

Skip the firefights, instead train your muscle for discipline. Like any other ability or trait, discipline is just a habit that can be learned, trained and strengthened.

Avoid the stress of last–minute and the mistakes and extra cleanup work of rushed deliverables. Get ahead of your tasks and priorities.

WEEK 28:
TAKE CONTROL, DON'T BURN OUT

Burnout comes from two key issues: the feeling that you cannot control what you need to work on (i.e., not being connected to ones' work) and the feeling that you can never get on top of  all the things you should be doing (i.e., the sense of not achieving).

Take control (or at least feel like you do). Consciously set your priority for the day.
Workaround things that control you and find the pockets where you can do the things that matter to you.
Set realistic goals and accept that there will always be unfinished work at the end of the day.

GAIN CONTROL OVER YOUR WORK

One of the most significant contributors to burnout (in my mind) is the feeling that you have endless tasks on your plate and not enough control over how you spend your time.

To a large degree, you can change that situation and feeling. Some of us have more control over our work lives, some less, but we can all find the pockets we can control and develop a mindset that helps us feel more 'on top of things.'

If you just go through your day and wait for others to dictate what you will be doing, you will very likely run into either boredom or burnout pretty quickly. Instead, get clarity on what is important to you, and what you need to do to achieve those outcomes or that kind of activities.

Set time aside for those activities as a 'passion–balance' for the work that gets pushed into your day by others. Even activities that get dictated by others can get a different spin if you approach them from a different angle. For example, you can look at an activity you need to do as just that, or you can see it as an opportunity to hone a specific skill of your's or teach others by developing best practices.

IT'S OK TO NOT GET TO THE BOTTOM OF YOUR TASK LIST

Chances are that you have more work that you should be doing than what you can fit into a realistic work day and work week.

List out the things that you need to do in priority order. Then assign realistic time to them. Knowing what needs to be done and how much time each task requires allows you to set <u>realistic</u> targets for the day and the week.

Work towards those targets and measure success against that specific set of pre-defined activities, not your complete list of things you should do.

As you work through your list, tick off everything that you have achieved, including the things that were dictated by others. Often when we are busy with lots of competing priorities and to-dos, we look back at the day and feel like we didn't accomplish anything. Having a list with lots of check marks helps you realize how much you have achieved.

KNOW WHAT YOU CAN CONTROL AND WHAT YOU CANNOT

Acknowledge when you get sidetracked by unplanned asks and firefights. Take them as priorities for the day and consciously count them as wins when you're done. They don't add to your existing priorities; they replace some of them. Don't try to achieve everything plus the added activities now.

Some days, all you can achieve is to deal with an escalation, even if you had planned differently. Other days, you can spend most of your time and your energy on the priorities you picked. Don't punish yourself by feeling bad in either case.

> "God, grant me the serenity to accept the things I cannot change, the courage to change the things I can, and the wisdom to know the difference."
> Serenity Prayer, Reinhold Niebuhr

WEEK 29:
MAKE QUICK DECISIONS AND EXECUTE THEM

I really like the Getting Things Done (GTD) framework. However, I think it's a little bit excessive in many parts. Here's my simplified version that I use every day.

Write it all down in one place. Prioritize and then block time to focus on the tasks that are most important. Rinse and repeat.

WRITE EVERY TASK DOWN AS IT COMES TO MIND

Write everything down so you don't have to worry about it anymore and won't spend mental energy on remembering it.

Use only one list. Otherwise, you will spend all your time looking for your task lists. I prefer electronic lists (Omnifocus)

since they are easy to group, reprioritize, and rearrange. However, paper works just fine as well — your choice.

Putting everything down right away frees your mind, saves you mental energy and lets you focus on what you're doing right now, not what you will need to do in the future.

It's also a nice feeling to tick off the things you have accomplished. Looking at a long list of completed and ticked off tasks is much more gratifying than hustling all day and being sure what you have done at the end of the day.

DO QUICK THINGS RIGHT AWAY

There's the 2 min rule: if something requires less than 2 mins to complete, do it right away. Don't write it down, don't postpone it for later, just do it.

The quick email response that only requires a short sentence – write it right away as you triage your emails. The grocery purchases that you bring into the kitchen – put them away, don't let them sit on the counter. Your dirty dishes – just put them in the dishwasher right after you finished your meal.

PRIORITIZE WHAT NEEDS TO GET DONE NOW

I'm sure there is a lot on your list. Everything is important, but not everything is equally important, and of the important things only a few are urgent.

Don't just do what you stumble upon on your list. Prioritize what needs to get done NOW. What is the most important thing right now? What can wait?

Also, be sure that you understand the difference between 'urgent' and 'important.' We can spend our whole life doing urgent stuff, but only little of that is really important looking back. Understand the difference.

Spend most of your time on important things, not the ones that seem urgent.

BLOCK TIME TO FOCUS ON IMPORTANT TASKS

Block time for the things that require time and focus. The things that you marked as important on your list. Pick the most important ones, assess how much you can achieve in a given time and then block that time. Don't just rely on doing them "some time this week." They are important, block the time.

You did the easy tasks right away (2 min rule), which means the remaining important task will require dedicated time. You will not magically find that time; you will need to make room for it.

REVISIT AND UPDATE YOUR PRIORITIES

You tick off many things from your list. At the same time, the importance or urgency of others will change. Your circumstances will change. If you're lucky, some of your tasks will even get solved by themselves.

As your priorities change, make it a point to revisit your list regularly. Update priorities as needed. Pick the list of things you want to accomplish in the next day or week and block time for them.

I do that exercise every Friday morning and go into the weekend with a clear plan of what's coming the next week. That frees my mind to focus on family and hobbies on the weekend rather than having to worry about what I might have forgotten at work.

HERE IS MY CHECKLIST FOR YOU: 'BEST OF GTD'

Organize and plan out

- Write down your tasks right away, so you don't need to worry about them anymore
- Prioritize once a week and decide which ones you're going to tackle

Do it, don't procrastinate and revisit (the 4Ds):

- **Do** – do it right away if it takes less than 2 mins or else plan some time to do it
- **Delegate** – if someone else should do it, delegate it right away, give the other person the opportunity to have time for the task
- **Defer** – if it's not important, defer it to a place that you revisit infrequently; chances are you will discard it the next time you revisit
- **Drop/discard** – if it's not important, discard the task; and don't feel bad about it

My own addition: Get clean Fridays

- Get to inbox zero on Fridays
- Schedule your calendar for the next week
- Prioritize your to-do list and pick what you want to tackle the following week

Then stop worrying for the weekend. Start the weekend clean and without work obligations.

WEEK 30:
INSIST ON FORWARD MOMENTUM

Few people like meetings. That's not because we don't like spending time with smart people; it's because most meetings don't move things forward. Instead, very often, they feel much more like energy and time drains. How often did you come out of meetings energized because you

felt that you had made a big step forward and now have a clear path to success?

Many of the meetings we find in our daily business routines are what I would call '**circular brainstormings**.' Instead of moving forward on a given topic in subsequent meetings, we tend to revisit previous assumptions and decisions and fall back into discussions we had already closed in the meeting before. That leads us to need another follow–up meeting to close out what we tried to accomplish in the first meeting but failed because we needed to spend too much time on baselining (again).

We all lose a LOT of time in those meetings.

CIRCULAR BRAINSTORMINGS

Circular brainstormings happen when:

- New attendees join the group and think they need to be caught up during the meeting at the expense of everyone else.
- Attendees don't remember what was discussed last time and need to reinvent definitions and previous decisions.
- It's unclear what the expected outcomes and deliverables of the meeting are, and the team tries to make them up on the fly.
- Everyone just has too much fun brainstorming and not much desire to get to the point where concrete action items and follow-ups will get assigned.

Circular brainstormings happen if we as leaders don't interject and force **'forward momentum.'** Groups have a tendency for circular brainstorming since it's a lot of fun, only requires much easier 'pie in the sky' dreaming and high–level what–ifs, instead of concrete action plans and ownership. Most importantly, it doesn't require a commitment to action.

Create forward momentum in every meeting. Document meeting outcomes and lock the baseline. Refuse to revisit decisions that were already made. Be deliberate about when you allow brainstorming.

FORWARD MOMENTUM

As leaders, we need to hold ourselves and our teams accountable to have meetings with **'forward momentum.'** I include myself, since unchecked, we all have the same tendencies.

A couple of things that help with 'forward momentum' are:

Protecting the baseline

When we exit a meeting, we made certain decisions and assumptions based on in-depth discussions. As we go into the follow-up meeting, we need to recap briefly and then fiercely protect that baseline. Unless there are earth-shattering new insights, we cannot reopen decisions, discussion, definitions that were previously locked. Forward momentum means building on what was established before, not starting all over again from scratch every single time. This also includes decisions that were made in other groups if the meeting is to define further details of a broader direction that was already set (if you were given a direction, don't reinvent the strategy).

Two-minute rule

We need to hold attendees accountable to be informed about what was discussed and decided before. If people are new, they can be caught up offline, but not at the cost of the group's time. We cannot have 20 people in a room to educate one person. If a discussion gets sidetracked because someone missed previously discussed topics, that catch–up needs to be taken offline unless it can be resolved in 2 mins (and those 2 mins include follow–up questions).

Know what success looks like

Every meeting needs to have an agenda. However, every meeting also needs to have clearly defined outcomes (unless it's an update meeting). What decisions will we have made at the end of the meeting? What artifacts will we have produced and shared at the end? Having those clearly defined outcomes can help to keep everyone on track and will keep the meeting owners accountable to maintain forward momentum.

Lock the baseline for the next meeting

To protect the baseline in the next meeting (see above), you first need to establish that baseline. At the end of each brainstorming and decision meeting, we need to be clear and explicit as to what we have decided and assume that as facts and truths for following meetings. We need to be clear as to what is still ambiguous and needs further investigation. We need to make two steps forward every time, not two steps forward and one step back.

Try it out! Be courageous and drive the meetings you attend forward. If you cannot break the loop and the group insists on circular brainstorming, pack your stuff, leave and do something productive.

WEEK 31:
LEARN TO COMPARTMENTALIZE

D o you know how CEOs, politicians, and leaders around the world keep all the balls in the air without going crazy? How can they fight fires all day without going crazy?

They learn to be good at compartmentalizing.

> Don't multitask, compartmentalize. Focus on the task at hand, then fully put it away when you move on to the next topic. Putting it away, locking it away is the key to compartmentalization.

Compartmentalizing is different from multitasking. If multitasking is the ugly villain, then compartmentaliz- ing is the super- hero.

Compartmentaliz- ing means doing a thing at a time fully. Without dis- traction, but then putting it away when you move to the next task and priority, the next topic, your next employee or the next firefight.

To focus on the topic at hand, you need to be able to put away everything else for the time being. Put it in their box, their compartment and don't worry about them until you deal with that compartment the next time.

Let go of thoughts and worries that want to spill over from your last topic and interaction.

It's hard to have that mental discipline, but it is the only way to stay focused on the topic, across multiple areas. It's also the only way to keep you sane.

Great leaders have perfected compartmentalization. They are able to have a challenging performance discussion with an employee, switch to an in-depth project discussion in the next meeting, and then back to a team celebration. They don't take baggage from previous interactions into the following ones.

However, compartmentalization is not just for CEOs. When you clean the house, don't think about shopping, when you spend time for yourself, don't worry about your to-do list, when you work with your kids, don't check your messages.

Don't forget all those other priorities; just put them away for the moment to prevent them from cluttering your focus and thinking.

Force yourself to compartmentalize. Resist the urge to multitask. Multitasking spreads you thin, compartmentalizing helps you stay focused and productive across many different areas that you have to deal with during the course of the day.

Compartmentalizing requires discipline and practice, but it keeps you sane.

WEEK 32:
BE THERE FULLY, OR DON'T BE THERE AT ALL

How often have you been in a meeting and didn't pay attention because you checked your email? Are you sitting at the dinner table with your loved ones and checking your phone? Are you working on a pro-

ject and continuously see reminders popping up?

What a waste of time for you and the ones who are with you.

Be in the here and now. Be in the moment.

If you do something, do it wholeheartedly. Don't waste your time and energy by being there without being present. Be respectful to others and their time. If this is not your priority and not worth your full attention, be honest, and don't do it.

Don't be in a meeting and do your email. In that case, it's way better to not go to the meeting to begin with. Focus. Don't waste your time with multi–tasking; it doesn't work.

Likewise, when you're with your family and friends, be with THEM. Don't check your Facebook or work email. You will regret not having focused on them when you look back a few years from now.

If you think something is not worth your time, attention, and energy, please have the courage to openly say so and don't come.

Experience your moments fully! Don't waste other's time.

WEEK 33:
THE POWER OF ROUTINE AND RHYTHM

PRESERVE YOUR WILLPOWER

We all have a certain amount of willpower available each day. Some days it's more because we are energetic, we slept well, or the sun is shining. Some days it's less.

Regardless of what our level is, every decision requires a little bit of that energy and depletes our will power for the day. When our willpower goes down, our ability to stick with priorities and resolutions goes down with it. When our willpower is depleted, it's harder to say 'no' to temptations and 'yes' to things that are good for us but require our conscious decisions and energy to get started.

That is why we drink alcohol after a challenging day, why we skip the gym in the evening if the day was stressful. The more our willpower is depleted, the less we can put in the way of not dropping on the couch, getting a bag of potato chips and a beer and watching TV.

> Manage your willpower carefully. Don't waste it for decisions that are not important. Create rhythms and stick to them.

Since our willpower is a limited resource, we need to manage and invest it carefully. We must not waste it for things that don't matter but focus it on the ones that do. The more we can remove unnecessary decisions or avoidable annoyances, the more we will be able to get the things that matter done.

SIMPLIFY DECISIONS

One powerful habit of avoiding wasting your willpower is to remove decisions that don't matter.

Here are some examples that don't matter on a day-by-day basis:

- When to get up in the morning – do it the same time every day
- What to eat for breakfast – you can celebrate that decision, but during the week, stick to one thing (for me it's an apple)
- Where to find your office stuff, keys, etc. – get it ready the evening before
- What to wear for work – I wear the same style every week, blue jeans, black long–sleeve shirt, sneakers; and I pack it on Sunday for the entire workweek
- What to eat for lunch – again, make it fancy on the weekend or in the evening, make it practical for lunch; I get soup and salad every day; it's healthy, gives me energy and isn't so heavy that I get tired
- Where to park – I park in the same spot every day; it's higher up in the garage, and I could be closer if I tried, but I waste zero energy finding a spot in the morning or wondering where my car is parked in the evening

I have many more things where I can go 'on autopilot' and still know I make the right decisions, but let's leave it there. You get the idea. Find out where you spend energy deciding every day, make the right decision once, then repeat and leave it there.

REMOVE ANNOYANCES

Reduce or remove things that deplete your willpower, even if it might mean you need to change your routines a little bit. It pays off as the day goes along.

Here are some examples of things that annoy me and what I do about them:

- Annoying traffic – move the times when you commute to avoid rush hour or take the bus; it's better to get up an hour earlier than to be stuck in traffic for 30 mins
- Distractions in the office – get good noise-canceling headphones, find a quiet place or work from home when you need to get things done
- People that don't give you energy or make you happy – ditch them; right now
- Spam calls on your phone – put it on mute and don't answer, you can always check your voice mail

Again, what is the list for you? What can you do to avoid those situations?

DECIDE AHEAD OF TIME

On the crucial decisions, it's best to decide before your willpower goes down. If you want to go to the gym in the evening, decide the day before and then execute. Don't hope you will make good decisions after a long day at work.

Create rhythms and triggers for those decisions, so you don't need to convince yourself every time. For example, put your gym bag on the driver seat of your car, so you have to see it when you leave work and get triggered to go.

DON'T STARVE YOUR WILLPOWER

Make healthy choices! Your brain needs glucose to fuel your willpower. When you're low on glucose levels, your willpower will shut down first. After all, for basic survival, willpower was the most dispensable investment. Don't think you're affected by that? How good are you at staying away from junk food, when you are starving?

Stay hydrated, but also keep your glucose levels at a constant level. Eat some fruit at regular intervals. Don't wait until you're hungry.

> There is power in rhythms and predictability. Build routines, build rhythms, and stick to them. Routines and rhythms give you structure, predictability, and peace of mind.

Don't wing it every single day, have a plan for what you want the day to look like. Whenever you can, stick to that plan. Be flexible and adjust but start from a good framework.

WEEK 34:
MAKE A PLAN TO CALM THE MONKEY MIND

In Zen our usual behavior is often referred to as the 'monkey mind.' Our mind is continuously busy, jumping from one thing to another, never entirely focusing on following through on any single priority. There is always another banana on the tree that grabs our attention.

> Calm your monkey mind. Reduce distractions.
> Make a plan and go for it.

Our goal is to calm the monkey mind. It is to remove distractions from our workplace, relationships, and life in general.

Our goal is to understand what's important today, the next week, this year and in our life. We need to assess, prioritize, and plan.

Our goal is to make time for those priorities and focus on them, without being distracted by the banana on the other tree.

Our goal is to empty your 'to do list chasing mind' and free it to concentrate on the work at hand.

This week is really about consciously bringing together all the pieces we discussed so far. Step back for a moment. Reflect on the things you practiced the last 30 weeks and make a plan on how you will bring them together.

Make a plan. Write it down. Commit to it.

Clear your mind, make a plan ahead. Stop your mind from wandering and worrying. However, also know that you won't fully stick to it and don't get frustrated when you don't.

PART III
SPIRITUAL BALANCE

At some point in time, the only thing that will matter is what you have left behind.

WEEK 35:
PUT ON YOUR OWN OXYGEN MASK FIRST

First we have focused on developing healthy habits to lay a sustainable foundation to go through our days. Then we explored ways to be more effective at work to free up time. Let's take both to good use and move on to exploring what really matters to you and then making time for those things – your purposes.

Put on your own oxygen mask first.

When you travel on any commercial airplane, you will need to go through the safety briefing before taking off. One of the things that stuck with me was the advice to "put on your own oxygen mask first."

It seems to go against our instincts initially. We want to help our kids or the elderly before we turn our attention to our own needs. However, that is shortsighted. If we're going to help others, we first need to take care of ourselves.

Let me repeat this – before we can help others, we need to take care of ourselves first!

In the specific example for airlines, there is no use in putting on the oxygen mask on your first child and then passing out before you can help the second. You have to get yourself into a stable spot before you can help others in a sustainable way. Put on your own oxygen mask first.

The same is true for less dramatic settings. You need to get yourself into a good spot first before you can have a positive impact on your family, friends, community, or society at large.

Get yourself a healthy basis, de-stress your work, find the things you care about, explore your passion, purpose, and spirituality, and allocate time and energy to it. Then help others and make this world a better place. This is what these tips, hacks, habits, and suggestions are all about.

Put on your own oxygen mask first.

Most likely the most crucial piece of advice of all.

WEEK 36:
ACCEPT YOUR WORRIES AND THEN TAKE ACTION

We all have our personal level of being worried; it actually doesn't change much with external circumstances. Some people are just happy–go–lucky, while others tend to always mull in the past and worry about the future.

Accept your worries. Then take action!

External events might push us up or down for a while, but surprisingly, we all bounce back to our personal levels, no matter how dramatic an incident happened to be. Death of a loved one is devastating, but usually, people move back to their previous  happiness level after a while. Winning the lottery is thrilling, but the glamor fades away quickly – as does the money in most cases.

TAKE ACTION

Accept and embrace your personal level of worries. It is just what it is. Work with your worries, embrace them, and take them as signals for things you can either improve in your current environment or at least mitigate.

However, don't day-dream and hope that all your worries will be magically solved if only that specific one thing would change (e.g., you get that promotion, you move to that new place, you quit that job,...).

Your worries will not change because of external events. They will only change because of the actions YOU take or mindset changes YOU make.

Fix your problems here and now and take them as opportunities to learn and grow. Don't hope for that external change that will make everything magically better.

Hope is a bad strategy.

BE IN THE HERE AND NOW

Most times, taking action is the right approach, but sometimes, you also need to change your perspective.

Mindfulness is a proven way to reduce your worries and increase your overall happiness. Observe the small things, like the taste and heat of the cup of coffee you hold in your hands. Enjoy the moment and the current pleasures, like the sun rays dancing on your face.

Be in the here and now.

Likewise, the people we are surrounded with influence our moods in a significant way. If you surround yourself with negative people, you will likely also develop a bleak view of the world. Change it. There are no brownie points for putting up with negative or rude people. Ditch them immediately and move on to greener pastures. If they happen to be family – do the same.

There are no free rides; people need to live up to being in your inner circle.

There are also times when an external change is needed. In those cases, move on and let go. At times, that's good and necessary. However, don't think that you will magically be a happier or better person if you don't change any of your inner parameters and attitudes along with it.

WEEK 37:
BE PART OF THE SOLUTION, NOT THE PROBLEM

You have three basic options to react when you are faced with a challenge, problem or just a frustrating situation: (1) you can hide your head in the ground and hope it goes away, (2) you can complain about it and become part of the problem, making it even worse or (3) you can find

ways to address and improve the situation, becoming part of the solution.

We already established that hope is a lousy strategy; hence, (1) is not a good path to follow. For obvious reasons, (2) is not any better, unless you are striving for a life of self–inflicted pain and misery.

> Don't be part of the problem. Be part of the solution.

So rather than dwelling in your pity, think about solutions you can bring to the table when you're faced with a severe or frustrating problem.

This happens to me every day. I go along with my day, and then out of the blue, I get that email which makes me want to choke someone's throat. Like everyone else, I get angry for a moment. However, I try to be conscious of that reaction, and then step back and think of other ways to react. Often I will take a few hours or even a good night sleep before I respond. That gives my subconscious mind some time to process and come up with a different perspective.

In Tai Chi, we say "there is always a third way." Usually, we only think about two reactions when confronted with an unpleasant situation: give in or fight back (fight or flight). There is always a third way through which you can turn the situation into something positive.

When faced with something that annoys you, don't give up, look away and walk away. Be part of the solution; find a creative way to solve the problem, drive that solution. Once your mission is accomplished, look back and be proud of how you reacted and what change you created.

When I am faced with something that makes my blood boil or makes me want to scream at someone, I give it a big pause first. Pretty much all problems can wait for a moment. A well thought through response and action plan is always better than a rushed one. Then I ask myself these three questions:

- What is the opportunity for change?
- How can I avoid or improve a similar situation in the future?
- How can I help others through situations like this?

I even have a Post–It sticker with those three questions on my office desk as a reminder.

I give it a moment or two. I find the third way, do what needs to be done and then move on. In every single case, I will be way more satisfied than if I had given in to my first impulses.

Whenever possible, try to identify the root cause of the initial issue and solve it so that the same situation won't happen again.

WEEK 38:
OPEN DOORS

I'm a person of lists and plans. I always want to have a plan for the short and longer term. I need to be organized to feel comfortable and be in control.

However, I was also taught by my teacher early on in my martial arts training, that situations constantly change and we need to adapt to new opportunities and challenges. As they say in the military: "all plans are outdated upon the first contact with the enemy."

Have a plan and follow it. However, watch out for unexpected opportunities and be flexible enough to change your plan to embrace them.

We need to have a plan and a goal to know where we want to go to, and to make progress towards that destination, instead of wandering aimlessly around ("going nowhere fast"). However, that plan must not make us myopic and oblivious for necessary change.

Throughout my life, I always had a plan, but the best things happened when an unexpected opportunity presented itself, and I reached out for it. Even though many times I was scared to my bones.

Having a plan and working towards it, prepares us to be ready for the moment when opportunities present themselves. However, if we don't make the leap and grasp them, all the preparation was for nothing.

Have a plan, work on it. Prepare yourself, but be ready to drop your plan and adjust to the moment when needed. Don't be scared of unexpected opportunities. They are when the magic happens in life.

I recently read a very similar idea in 'Racing Winter on the Pacific Crest Trail,' by Kyle S Rohrig. It goes like this:

There are always doors that open unexpectedly for us. Walk through them. After you walk through an open door, new doors will open up behind, eventually leading to an endless universe of open doors and opportunities. You find good thing behind open doors.

If you close the door, the opportunities end right there. That's it, end of the story, you're stuck. Being stuck is stagnation. Stagnation is the beginning of the end.

In the words of Daoism:

> When we are young we are flexible, we push out, we try new things and grow. When we stop being curious and flexible, we get hard. When we get hard, we break, crumble and fade away.

Be open, be flexible, see opportunities!

WEEK 39:
BE HOME WHEN YOU'RE HOME

W hat is the most essential part of your life? What will be the one thing that remains when everything weakens and fades away (like your career, your friends and eventually your health)?

It's your family. Your family is the one thing that won't go away – that is unless you screw it up.

Work hard at the office. Be home when you're home. Disconnect. Develop a shutdown routine for the transition.

Work hard at the office. Follow your hobbies and passions. But not at the expense of the time you spend with and invest in your family.

You will not be able to get back the time that you have wasted. When your par-ents left this world, they will be gone. Anything you didn't say until then will remain unheard forever. If you don't bind with your kids while they are young and looking up to you, chances are they will not care much about you once they are grown up and independent.

The family should be your single most important priority. Then come health and your wellbeing (put on your own oxygen mask first). After that follow your passions. Everything else comes after.

WHEN YOU'RE HOME BE HOME

Work hard at the office but then turn everything off and mentally disconnect on your way back home. When you're home, be home! Don't check back on messages or return phone calls. Don't fret over your problems at work; you won't solve them that evening anyway. Tomorrow is another day. Often problems are solved over a good night sleep, as we grant our subconscious brain the freedom to go where it needs to go without our interference.

DEVELOP A SHUTDOWN AND TRANSITION ROUTINE

Turn everything off when you leave your office. Develop a shutdown routine to help yourself disconnect from work worries. Shutdown routines can be anything from closing your books, tidying up your work desk or shutting down your computer. Make it a routine though, and over time it will automatically trigger your brain into the right state.

Further the mental transition on your commute. Drop work thoughts and get into family thoughts. Do this even if it's just from room to room for folks who work at home. The physical separation between work and family helps a lot. If you do work at home, be sure to have a place for work and a place for family. If you are a stay at home parent, don't make the place where you gather and play in the evening, the place where you do your chores.

When you're home be home. Don't check emails, check in with your family and friends!

WEEK 40:
HAVE DINNER WITH FRIENDS AND FAMILY

We already talked about the importance of spending time with family and friends. One great and proven way to do that is by sharing meals.

There is plenty of science, as well as just age-old experience, that sharing meals serves a strong bonding function.

> Share meals with friends and family. Talk about the day, thoughts, dreams, and worries. Make it a priority every day.

Share meals with your teams, friends, and family. Cook together or go out to eat together. While you're sharing food, spend time talking and laughing. Play games, listen to the stories of the day.

Make this a priority every day.

Do NOT check your messages, play with your phone or read the news. Mealtime is 'together time.' Value the time others spend dining with you by giving them your full attention.

If you want to bond with your kids and share your values and priorities with them, it is critically important to share meals. Those occasions allow for catching up on the day in a relaxed environment, sharing ideas, thoughts, passions, and even worries that might otherwise go unnoticed.

Studies have shown that sharing meals is critical for the healthy development of children. Leaving food in the fridge and having everyone snack at different times just doesn't cut it.

WEEK 41:
FOCUS ON EXPERIENCES, NOT STUFF

We're living in the age of consumerism, in which most people see the purpose of their lives in accumulating stuff. However, instead of gathering stuff, following the latest marketing fad or competing with your neighbors, you should invest in experiences.

> Invest in experiences, not stuff. Plan for experiences and then make it a point to follow–through on them. If you are too tired when it's go-time, do them anyway.

Most stuff won't make you happy beyond the rush of the purchase. In many cases, it's even worse, with buyer's remorse kicking in just a few hours later. The gadget that you so badly needed often ends up sitting in a drawer after only a few uses.

Instead, invest in experiences. Preferably experiences that are shared with friends and family. Experiences create memories, and memories stay with you forever.

You can always come back to memories to pick you up when you're down. Looking at last year's cool gadget won't have the same effect.

The additional benefit of investing in experiences is also that the positive effect is not limited to the time when you have the experience.

THE THREE PHASES OF AN EXPERIENCE

Planning

We enjoy the preparation of an experience that we are looking forward to. We can derive fun from the excitement weeks and months before we even take off. I usually plan summer vacations in the dark months of winter. It feels good to think about upcoming adventures and helps to pass rainy days.

Doing

The experience is, of course, the fun part. At times it can be challenging and exhausting as well, but that's ok. The more challenging an experience is, and the more it pushes us to the limits of our comfort zone, the more memorable and positive it usually is. You only value something if you had to work hard for it.

Remembering

The last part of an experience stays with you forever – your memories. You can relive an experience as often as you want. No one can take it away from you. You can look back at pictures, recount stories with your partners in crime, make a photo book, or plan to repeat the experience at some time in the future.

DO IT ANYWAY

One last advice on experiences, from the book 'Off the Clock' by Laura Vanderkam: even if you're tired and just want to sit on the couch when the time to venture off on your experience comes – do it anyway.

> "Plan it in. Do it anyway."
> Laura Vanderkam, Off the clock

While we get excited planning for an experience, once the day approaches, we are often so worn down and tired that we just want to plop down and turn on the TV. Resist the urge! Go anyway. Get yourself over the hump; it will be worth it!

Plan for your experience and when it's time to get going, go. No matter what. Plan it in. Do it anyway! You will be glad you did it.

Invest in buying time, experiences, and life memories. They are preferably shared with loved ones. Leave your kids with memories and experiences, not stuff that they will need to throw away later.

WEEK 42:
BUY FEWER THINGS BUT THINGS THAT YOU REALLY LIKE

No, I'm not a monk. I possess things, and I take pleasure from working with and using tools and gadgets that I really care about.

Have fewer things, but things that you really value.

What I learned and changed over time is to have fewer things, but things that I value.

When I was a boy, my dad always told me to spend my money on fewer things that are higher quality and will last and give me pleasure longer. As in so many cases, I should have listened to him closer. It took me  many years to relearn the same lesson on my own.

How many different jackets do you need versus having a few that you want to wear every day? Do you need all those different gadgets versus a phone and tablet that you really like? How many different shoes do you need to own? How much silverware do you need? How much stuff to decorate your home? How many stuffed animals? How big does your house have to be? How many cars do you need? What are you going to do with that bigger property?

The more stuff you have, the more your mind and life get cluttered. Also, the more stuff you have, the more time, energy, and money you will need to manage and maintain that stuff. The more stuff you have, the more of your time you will spend with the things that you don't like as much or feel guilty that you don't, and the less time you will spend with the things that give you joy.

I developed a process to deal with shopping urges. When I get excited about a new gadget, I will read all about it and then put it on my Amazon wish list. That's already half of the gratification with nothing spent so far. I will have it sit on that wish list for a while and only if I still think after a few weeks that I need that gadget I will buy it. In most cases, I end up deleting it from my list.

You don't need to become a monk. However, do focus on fewer things that give you real joy. Instead, spend more money on fewer high-quality items that you love dearly than the same amount on a lot of stuff that you don't care about much.

Even better, invest in things that help you create experiences rather than things that sit on your shelf.

Also, remember that many things that create experiences can be rented rather than bought. It takes many boat trips to warrant the purchase of a motorboat.

WEEK 43:
SIMPLIFY AND DECLUTTER

We already talked about focusing on your priorities, cleaning up your calendar and inbox and decluttering your workspace. Let's now take a broader stab at simplification and decluttering.

> Simplify and declutter. Do it quick and radically; it will develop inertia. Don't limit decluttering to your physical space; do it everywhere. Don't fill up the empty space with new stuff.

Simplification helps you be you more relaxed, in the moment and happier because you are distracted by fewer things. There's less stuff to maintain or to worry about. Further, clean space allows your mind wander freely and come up with new  ideas, while stuff distracts and captures it (often with all the things you still have to do, like dusting those vases).

SIMPLIFY AND DECLUTTER RADICALLY

Simplification and decluttering (i.e., the art of getting rid of things you don't need) gains momentum as you are doing it. It has strong inertia in either direction.

It's pretty hard to get started. Off the top of your head, you seem to need all the things you have – why else would you have bought them in the first place?

However, push through it. Once you identified a few things that you don't need anymore, or never truly enjoyed having in the first place, things will get easier. As you get rid of things, you will feel relief, and that will propel you to get rid of more things that you don't really need or want anymore.

Be willing to cut deep and cut fast. Putting one thing away a week will not give you that momentum and positive feedback. Instead, take a weekend afternoon and make it a goal to fill a whole moving box (or two if you are an ambitious person). Don't fret over decisions; if you don't want to fight for an object, you are probably ready to let go.

CUT YOUR LOSSES

There's a rule in investing that applies here as well:

Don't throw good money after bad money.

What that means is that you should not add additional money to a sub-par investment only because you hope that it will get better in the future. While that stock that went down for a year is cheap now, the chances are that the trend will continue and you will lose much money.

Likewise, if you have bought something in the past that seems like a less stellar idea today, don't get stuck in that 'investment.' It might have been a good idea back then, but if it is not anymore, then say goodbye. Don't throw 'good money' (your time, energy, and mental capacity) after 'bad money' (something you don't care about anymore).

If you have separation anxiety, don't throw things away or donate them right away. Put them in a box. Once you didn't touch that box for three months, bring it to a local charity for donation.

It's ok to have bought something that doesn't fit your life anymore. Cut your losses.

ONE AREA AT A TIME

Attack one area of simplification at a time. Don't let yourself get distracted as you hop from area to area.

If you want to declutter your living room, don't get distracted as you bring stuff out through the garage. Pick one area or room at a time and tune out everything else. As always: focusing wins the day!

Decluttering and simplification are not only about stuff. The space you live in has a big part, but clutter and complexity are everywhere. Address all those spaces:

- **Spaces** – your home and living spaces, your yard, your office and workspaces, you storage (how much of that stuff do you need),...
- **Obligations** – emails, calendar, volunteering, promises to 'friends,' events,...
- **Digital** – websites, news, games, (phone) apps,...
- **Relationships** – friends that don't lift you up, connections that drag you down, negative people, 'friends' on social networks,...

DON'T FILL UP THE EMPTY SPACE

Of course, once you have decluttered an area, don't fill up the empty space with new stuff. Keep the emptiness and enjoy it.

A clean empty space is not an invitation to bring in lots of new stuff (new clutter).

Cherish it, protect it, feel bad for anything that contaminates it. Regard anything that moves into that space as an intruder who needs to fight for its right to be there.

WEEK 44:
COME BACK TO YOURSELF

Who is the most critical person in your life? It's you. It has to be you!

You might be as altruistic as you may, you always have to take care of yourself first. "Put on your own oxygen mask first."

Make time to meet yourself. Plan in me-time. Experiment and find the best way to connect with yourself.

TAKE TIME FOR YOURSELF

There is no way you can take care of yourself if you don't slow down every now and then and make time for it. Embrace the downtimes and slow down. We grow from stress and relieve, not from constant stress.

COME BACK TO YOURSELF

Not every method works for every person the same.

What is the best way for you to get back in touch with yourself? Experiment with different methods and find out what works best for you.

- **Mindfulness** – Spend a few minutes with mindfulness, giving your attention to every single detail of a given experience, as mundane as eating a piece of fruit.
- **Walk outside** – Go outside for a walk in nature and experience all the sights, sounds, and smells that present themselves.
- **Meditate** – Do some meditation, Yoga, or Tai Chi. Listen to your breath. Watch your thoughts come, and then send them away again onto their journey.

Embrace the Yin and Yang. Most times of the day, we are high-powered and push through our days, entirely externally focused. Balance that external orientation with deliberate 'me' time. Experiment what works for you.

WEEK 45:
GET INSPIRATION

J ust as our body needs food and nutrients, our mind needs inspiration. We usually get that inspiration from being exposed to new experiences, information, and stimuli. The more we work in our comfort zone of the things we already know and the routines we already master, the less our minds are

challenged, inspired, and nurtured.

Seek out new experiences that challenge your existing beliefs. Nurture your mind. Get inspired and work hard for new insights instead of being dulled by passive consumption.

Treat yourself with new stimuli every day. Opt for active experiences and information over passive consumption. Active stimuli are those that you need to process and work for like learning a craft. Passive stimuli are those that you can mindlessly consume like watching TV.

Ditch your TV (we did that many years ago and never regretted it), delete your computer games, limit your social media times.

Instead seek experiences that extend what you already know, push your boundaries, and challenge your comfort zone.

There are many ways to stimulate and inspire yourself. Pick a few and make time for them. Pick a fixed time in your day or week that is devoted to those experiences and inspirations to make sure you prioritize them.

Reading

Read a non–fictional book about an area that interests you, or even a completely new topic. Read a chapter every day and reflect on it.

Learning a craft

Learn a new craft or a new hobby. Push yourself to learn and grow all the time. Maybe your job provides those opportunities, if it doesn't, either seek out new challenges in your work or find them in your personal time.

Pursuit of mastery

Push for mastery in something that you are passionate about. Find something that excites you longterm and go deeper and deeper, exploring the core ideas and concepts (for me it's my martial arts journey that kept me exploring and discovering for over 25 years now).

Different perspectives

Talk to interesting new people and try to understand their views. This is not about talking to the same people you already know and meet all the time. Those are often echo chambers, only confirming what you already believe. Instead, seek out new perspectives and opinions and reflect on them. Avoid negative people though; they are not worth the negative impact they will have on you.

Seek surprises

Expose yourself to situations that surprise you. Travel. Seek out new experiences. Change your context and challenge your frameworks. Break complacency whenever it creeps up.

WEEK 46:
GO OUTSIDE INTO NATURE

F ind some time to get out into nature!

Science has shown that getting out into nature regularly boosts your health and mental wellbeing. Make it a point to spend time in nature regularly.

Get out into nature. The less manicured, the better. Pay attention to what you see, to the smells and sounds. Breathe! Live!

Walk your dog, hike, bike, or play with your kids outside. Tend to your garden or backyard, get your hands dirty with soil. Whatever gets you going, do it. If you can't get yourself to walking regularly, buy a dog.

Make it walking time in nature, though, not the concrete deserts of the city. Human beings are animals at their cores. We need nature, we need the green, and we need to see some natural messiness. Parks are ok, but the more natural 'wilderness' you can find, the better.

Find trees, mosses, green, and dirt. Go out in nature and explore the small and big wonders.

There seems to be a fancy new term and movement for everything these days. Naturally, there is also a fancy Japanese way of walking in the woods. It's called Shinrin-yoku (森林浴), and really only means to walk in the forest, be mindful of what you encounter and watch your breath. I leave it to you to decide if you need a Shinrin-yoku instructor or just some sturdy boots. I opt for the latter, but I'm also a simple person.

Go low-key (dog walking) or fancy (Shinrin-yoku, forest bathing), whatever meets your needs, but do it!

WEEK 47:
MAKE TIME FOR CREATIVITY

We are all creative, and we enjoy, even crave expressing ourselves through that creativity. You might not know, but you are creative as well. It might be painting, writing, making music, sculpting, writing poems, working with flowers or gardens. Whatever it is, find the creative expression that is yours and embrace it.

Identify your creative passion. Embrace it. Block time. Have a regular date with your creativity. Don't do it for anyone other than yourself.

For the longest time (about 50 years), I thought I didn't have any creative talents or passions in me. Then one day it dawned on me, that I enjoy writing. Moreover, I have done it in one way or another my whole life, starting from early childhood. I have

not given it the space it deserved or the acknowledgment I should have, but I've subconsciously done it anyway.

For Uli it's painting and flower arrangements, for our seven-year-old son it's building stuff, and our daughter is just writing on her first horse book at the age of nine (she only has about ten pages so far, but that's not the point).

Find out what fuels your creativity. If you already know, awesome. If you don't, experiment. Try things out. Take a few classes. See what sticks.

Not knowing and exercising your creative passions leaves a significant gap in your life.

Once you identified your creative passion, make time for it! Whether you block an hour every day, a few evenings during the week, or some time on Saturday and Sunday doesn't matter. What matters is that you book that time with yourself and stick to it. Make an appointment. Have a date with your creativity.

Enjoy witnessing as you create something new that you are passionate about. Most important, don't worry about others. All that matters is what you think about your works and how you feel about the outcome.

As I'm writing this, I'm sitting on a deck, in the sunshine, on a trip to Germany. The whole family is taking a nap while I can indulge in my creativity, writing down these thoughts.

'An audience of one' is a great book to explore that thought a little more.

Whatever it is for you, writing, painting, music, photography – do it, make it a point in your life!

WEEK 48:
PRACTICE MINDFULNESS

You hear people talking about 'mindfulness' a lot these days. Some of it is hype, but it also is for a good reason. For centuries philosophers, artists and monks have stressed the importance of being in the moment. Of fully living in the 'now.' One fundamental Zen principle is to 'be in the here and now.'

Be in the here and now.

Mindfulness has many benefits to offer. It helps us be better at what we are doing because we give it our full focus. It helps to calm our mind because we don't get distracted and torn between many things at the same time. More-over, it helps us to be happier be-cause we put our full attention to the moment and  with that have more profound and more satisfying experiences.

Uli teaches mindfulness for kids at our Elementary School, and it helps kids who are struggling with their attention to re-center and managing their emotions better. What she does are very simple exercises, but they have a strong and hopefully lasting impact on those kids.

Put some mindfulness into your life as well. That does not at all mean that you need to book fancy classes or expensive coaches. It much rather means to simplify your thinking and to bring it back to the details of the current moment.

FOCUS ON THE TASK

What are you doing right now? What precisely? Are you on autopilot? If so, turn it off and go manual. Bring your attention back into what you're doing. Deliberately execute every single step of your current task

EXPERIENCE THE ENVIRONMENT

What sensations are you exposed to? What do you see, hear, feel, and smell? Is it cold or warm right now? What is the feel, weight, and texture of the tool you are using right now? What smells and sounds are in your environment?

TUNE IN TO YOUR BODY

How is your body feeling? Do you have tensions anywhere? Are you standing or sitting upright or slouching down? Are you smiling or frowning? Remember, your outside reflects on your inside; your posture reflects on your mood.

LISTEN TO YOUR BREATH

Your breath is your most straightforward but most powerful and essential tool. First of all, without proper breathing, you will die in minutes. Further, your breathing controls your mood, your stress level and even hormone levels like adrenaline. Learn to breathe deliberately and consciously. Learn to listen to your breathing. Learn to control your breathing and to let your breathing control your mindset. Start by just listening, then expand to gently controlling and adjusting the speed and pattern of your breathing.

MINDFUL EXERCISES

Some exercises help you to be in the moment. Tai Chi is known for that effect, meditation as well. Yoga can get you there if you do it right. Most martial arts, taught by a true teacher, will lead your there as well. Running on the treadmill and watching the news or reading won't. Those are good for cardio, but if you exercise distracted, you miss out on the awareness and mindfulness. I even stopped listening to music while I'm running on the trail. I loved it, but listening to the sounds of nature and feeling the gravel under my barefoot running shoes is even better.

> Be mindful of what you do – every moment and every little detail of it!

WEEK 49:
ENGINEER YOUR HAPPINESS, COUNT YOUR BLESSINGS

How you perceive your world and look at opportunities is much more influenced by your mindset than by your circumstances. External events will affect your happiness at the moment, but after a short time, you will bounce back to your 'natural' level.

The good news is that we can train our mental frameworks and over time, change our perspective on the things we encounter in daily life. We can make ourselves happier and more positive human beings. Moreover, by making ourselves more positive, we will face more encouraging situations and as a result, follow more fulfilling opportunities.

WORST DAY OF MY LIFE

Every night at the dinner table, we do a little round robin where everyone talks about the experiences of the day. It took our kids a while to get there, but now they love it and can't wait to tell their story.

For a while, our seven-year-old son had a phase where he always started with "the worst day of my life." For some reason, he thought it was cool, but we could see how it always dragged him down emotionally.

We can observe the same in us. As grownups, we often look back at how hard a day was, all the things that went wrong, all the annoying interactions.

With that, we train our brain to pattern match. If we pay attention to something, our mind will look for more of the same and proudly present it to us. When you think about buying a new car, you will all of a sudden see that model everywhere.

Indulging on the things that were bad or went wrong will train your brain only to see things going wrong. It's a self–fulfilling prophecy.

CHANGE YOUR MENTAL FRAMEWORKS

Instead of thinking back to what went wrong in your day, spend time every day to reflect on what was great, fun, or just positively memorable. You can do this throughout the day or in the evening before you go to bed. However, do it every day!

Reflect on the positive things that happened every day. Write them down.

Focusing on the positive things will train your brain to pattern match for those. It will help you see the good more easily and more often. It will help you see the opportunity to get more of those positive interactions. It will make you happier and more successful.

I bought a little notebook for myself in which I write down three positive things that happened to me every day. It's a great exercise to reflect and boosts your happiness.

We also changed our dinner routine and added the question "What were your three most positive things today?" before we get into talking about our days. Our kids are fighting for who can share those first and usually end up with more than three.

I also haven't heard the "worst day of my life" sentence anymore.

Being happy is in your control. So is being unhappy. You decide.

WEEK 50:
EXPLORE YOUR PURPOSE

W hat is your purpose? What makes you get up in the morning? What keeps you going when the going gets tough?

Understand your values and purpose. Then take a critical look at what you are doing right now. Be willing to experiment and take risks. Always keep your eyes open for opportunities that present themselves.

THE PASSION TRAP

In many ways, we are overemphasizing purpose and passion today. We tell High school kids that they need to find their passion when they pick

a career. An impossible task at that age. Many people actually never discover what their passion really is.

Doing something, that you are sufficiently interested in, with full dedication until you head towards mastery often turns into passion. This is, in fact, a more likely way to find something that you will be passionate about, than soul–searching for the perfect occupation.

Passion doesn't come magically for free. It requires dedication and hard work.

ALIGNMENT WITH CORE VALUES COUNTS

However, at the same time, too many of us spend our lives in settings, that go against our core values and our purpose. We do things and execute work that we don't agree with in principle.

Both trying to find the one thing that will make you happy just by its nature as well as sticking with something that fundamentally disagrees with your core values and purpose are futile.

It is much better to understand what your core values and purpose are, and then experimenting with different things. Once you find something that aligns in principle and piques your interest, go deep and give it your full self.

What makes you tick

Self-reflection and self-awareness are not easy. For some of us, it comes more naturally; others never find it.

If you are not clear about what inherently motivates you and what turns you off, you can start journaling your mini–motivators. Throughout the day, what did you like, what felt great, and what didn't? When you watch other people, what do you admire and what do you despise. What would you want other people to say about you, and what would you rather not?

Those should be small and in–the–moment things. Don't overthink it. Jolt down the random reactions and thoughts as they come, for example, "those meetings as sapping out my energy," "it felt really good to help Joe through his problem" or "it was awesome to solve this situation my way."

After a few weeks look at those micro–motivators and see what patterns emerge.

Brainstorm on new options

Then reflect on how much those value and purpose patterns are matched in your current occupation. If they are not, make a list of other careers that would get you to a closer match. Don't go for a perfect match; chances are you won't find that (lucky you, if you do!).

Make a list of those close matches and be aware that you will still have to work hard for them. Nothing will be rosy all day every day. Just setting expectations here.

MAKE A CHANGE, REINVENT YOURSELF

Let's assume that your values and passions don't align well with your current occupation. That's nothing to feel wrong about. For one, it's super hard to find proper alignment from the get-go. In most cases, we don't know enough about the job as well as ourselves when we begin. Also, we are (luckily!) changing over time and what might have been the perfect milestone a few years ago, might not fit any more as our path leads us to the next one.

Start experimenting with the occupations that made it to your list, or something completely different that feels right for reasons that you cannot explain.

If we talk about significant shifts in your occupation and trajectory, really experiment. Don't go full in right away without really knowing if you like where you're heading. Try out a few things on the side. Volunteer in the new occupation rather than leaving your current job only to figure out after a few months that the grass isn't greener on the other side.

EXPERIMENT, BE FLEXIBLE

Experiment a lot. Learn from those experiments. Adjust what you know about yourself and tweak the list of things you want to do based on that knowledge.

Recognize open doors and opportunities as they present themselves and find the courage to explore them.

Don't put yourself under the stress of having to succeed with the first thing you try out.

One of the life lessons I learned from my martial arts teacher was to have a plan but remain flexible.

> Have a plan, but always keep your mind open for opportunities that present themselves. Have the flexibility and courage to leverage them. Life is a winding path, not a straight line.

Looking at my winding path, I can point out at least four rather significant shifts in the direction I was heading. Each turn has set me back a little in the short-term – as significant change always does – but propelled me toward a much better place in the long-term. I don't even want to imagine who I would be if I had been stuck in my initial (subsequent, current) choices.

WEEK 51:
HAVE IMPACT BEYOND YOURSELF

We talked a LOT about what we can do to balance and improve our lives. Of course, life is much bigger than just us. Once we got our own house in order, we need to impact others positively.

Make positive ripples in the big pond of life. Watch them spread out.

Think of it as throwing a rock into a calm surface of water. We are the rock, the ripples that are created are the positive impact and change that we create. They spread out from us to every corner of the pond. They might get smaller in the distance,  but they will still reach out and transfer the message.

TEACH YOUR KIDS WELL

Our time on this planet is limited. We can start positive change, but very soon we will need others to pick it up and continue the journey for us. Invest time in preparing the passing of the baton.

Teach your children well. Set positive examples. Love them and also show them the boundaries they need to grow up. Help them become capable of dealing with the challenges they will face on their own.

Don't forget, though, that there is a lot we can learn from our children as well. Watch them closely and see what lessons they might have for you. Watch their curiosity, get inspired by their eagerness to explore the world.

Teach them in their own language, and just every once in a while, try to see the world through their eyes.

If you don't have children on your own, look at your extended family. Look at your community. Volunteer for coaching.

You have learned a lot in your life, pass it on through positive example and influence. Don't let it go wasted.

HELP YOUR COMMUNITY OR SOCIETY

The next ripple in the pond is your community and in extension, the larger society.

You don't need to become a politician to have a positive impact. I might even argue that your chance of having a positive impact is much more significant if you are not a career politician.

Engage in your neighborhood, in your school, at your local senior center. Find a cause that you care about and make a little difference.

I try to help people by teaching Tai Chi, mindfulness, compassion, and sharing some of the lessons I have learned in my career. Uli volunteers as an art docent and helps challenged kids at the school with breathing, calming, and mindfulness exercises. Find the cause you care about and then share it with others.

If you don't find yourself to be altruistic, you might consider countless scientific studies that have shown that we get more satisfaction from doing good to others than from splurging ourselves. Help others to help yourself.

Be the change agent for your community. It will spread out. Just help someone without expecting a return. Just say a happy 'hello' with a smile to a stranger and let yourself be surprised by what will happen.

ENVIRONMENTAL IMPACT

Last not least, we need to take care of the planet we live on. We started our discussion by taking care of our own health. Let's close the loop and also take care of the health of our planet.

We cannot survive without our planet, the animals, and plants that inhabit it with us. We need to find a healthy balance with our environment.

Don't consume more than you need. Don't waste food, water, or other resources. Don't litter. Don't destroy unnecessarily.

We just borrowed this planet. Let's make sure to give it back in good shape.

WEEK 52:
HIKE YOUR OWN HIKE!

U p to now we have talked about many new habits and behaviors to live healthier, be more effec- tive at our jobs, and give more time to our spiritu- ality. We gave you many suggestions and frameworks to balance your lives.

TRY IT; THEN ADOPT IT AND MAKE IT YOURS

Try them out and see what works for you. Then sit back and reflect. Use what works, change, and adapt what doesn't and discard what feels wrong. It needs to be about you. I know what works for me; I cannot know and prescribe what works for you.

There are two martial arts teachings that reflect this well. One is an old principle for teaching martial arts:

> The teacher shows the door. The student needs to walk through it on their own.

The other is my favorite quote from the famous founder of Aikido, Morihei Ueshiba:

> "Learn and forget."
> Morihei Ueshiba, founder of Aikido

Don't blindly follow gurus and role models, or what I am writing in this book. All of those are inputs, suggestions, food for thought. Only you can find out what works for you. No one else can do that for you.

Learn new ways. Try them out until you understand them. Then forget the rules and let your intuition kick in. Be surprised and amazed by what will unfold.

WHAT YOU 'CAN' VERSUS WHAT YOU 'WANT'

Be careful to understand what you WANT to do. Often we just keep doing what we're doing because we became reasonably good at it.

For example, I like to help others. I see where I can pitch in and make others great while also making a great living for myself. I am good at working in big IT companies, managing complex projects and products. However, is it what I really want? That is a question that I need to check in with myself regularly and get to an honest answer.

It's too easy just to keep doing what you're good at. To just follow the inertia of the path you started on when you were a different person all those years ago after High School.

I'm not saying you need to change your path. I'm saying though, that you need to be conscious and deliberate about it. Don't just let it happen. When it's time, find the courage to reinvent yourself.

> Be careful to differentiate between what you can do, what is the natural next step to do (inertia) and what you really want.

FIND YOUR OWN WAY

Once you know what works for you and you know what path you want to follow, go there. Blaze your own trail, or as they say in the hiker community: "Hike your own hike."

Be courageous. Don't look at others for models or confirmations. Invent your path as you push forward. "Boldly go where no man has gone before." (You have to find where that reference comes from... ☺)

Hike your own hike!

MASTER CLASS: REFLECTIONS ON ACHIEVING YOUR GOALS

Busy is not successful. Know where you want to go and how to get there.

A SPECIAL NOTE ON BURN OUT

We talked about different aspects and approaches to increase efficiency and control of your priorities. Those habits are useful for anyone, but consciously and consistently applying them is even more critical if you are working in an environment that is high stress or even conducive to burnout.

Burnout creeps on you, and it is not pretty when it gets you. It also takes much more effort to cure it than to prevent it. In the following, I'll provide a shortlist of principles that  have worked for me in such situations in the past. They won't work universally, but some of them might do the trick for you. If you feel stressed right now, give them a try and see what they can do for you.

I initially called those ideas 'hacks' to sound trendy, but changed it to 'principles' to make a point: those are not quick and easy fixes. You need to be serious, deliberate, and consistent about them. You have to put in the energy to make them work. Moreover, you need to keep doing it every day.

My principles will move on a spectrum from purpose (to keep your passion and happiness) to time management (to make room for all that purpose stuff).

PROTECT YOUR PERSONAL PASSIONS

The most critical rule comes first:

> Know what you care about outside of work. Set
> time for those activities. Block it on your calendar
> and then protect it fiercely.

It is crucial to create a balance between your work and your passions outside of work. There is always more to be done at work, thus tending to slowly creep into your personal life to the point where you suddenly realize that something is fundamentally wrong. Death by a thousand paper cuts. Don't let that happen.

Know what's important to you and then create rules to protect it. Those rules need to be yours. Different things work for different people.

For me, family comes first. With that, I have a rule that I don't work once I'm home. I don't work on weekends. I might come in early or stay later if I need to, but when I'm home, I'm home. There are a few cases where I deliberately decide that I want to finish something on the weekend, but I have a very high bar for those exceptions.

CREATE THE MOMENTS YOU CARE ABOUT AT WORK

We talked about making time for your passions. The same applies to your work passions:

> Don't get lost in tactical work. Set focus times
> where you do the things that matter to you and
> that align with your passion.

We all chose our jobs for a reason. We chose them because we are deeply passionate about core components of the role. At the same time, every job comes with a bunch of things we are not quite as excited about: the routine, the day to day, the reactive.

We need to do those things, but we must make sure that we don't get lost in them and forget what excites us. Just as for your passions, you must block time for the things that get you excited at work. Again, it's very personal to you what that is, but make sure it doesn't get lost in the daily 'rat race.'

For me, my primary motivators are working with and coaching great people. I also love to solve problems and build products. I'm blocking time for those deliberately. Being a data guy, I even color code my calendar to get reminded every time I look at my schedule if I'm striking a balance that works for me.

CHANGE YOUR MINDSET

We all have to do things we don't particularly care about much. After all, we're not at a party; we get paid to do a job for our company. However, usually, there is a reason for the things we do:

Try to understand the reason. Discover the meaning. It makes a huge difference!

There is a reason for everything. While specific tasks might seem tedious and unnecessary, in most cases, they serve an essential and distinct purpose.

For example, at Amazon, we write many documents, and we continuously look at a lot of data. Very often, I see the question "why do we need to do this" in people's eyes. There is a reason. Looking at data helps you understand what's going on, reflect, and learn what happened and why. Then you can develop the right action plan to correct what you're doing moving forward. Writing documents helps to sharpen your thinking and then to sell your ideas to others to get the proper support to make them happen.

If you look at the real purpose of why things are done, you can find much more satisfaction in doing them. There is ample research that purpose and passion are not defined by what you do, but how you think about it.

PACE YOURSELF

Sometimes we have to push hard and go late. Make sure you don't make it 'always.'

> There are times when you need to push hard and give it your all (and maybe more). However, there are also times when you can recharge your batteries a little. Know when you need to do which.

It's essential to understand when you need to push hard and when you don't. None of us can go full throttle all the time over an extended period of time.

Push hard when you need to, but also recognize when you have a period where you can recharge batteries. This is not about slacking because that will only catch up with you. It's about knowing when you have to do 120% and when 90% is just fine. Remove the pressure from yourself when you can and don't feel bad about it.

When I have the occasional day, when I can go home at 4 pm and enjoy a sunny evening with my family, I cherish that time and don't feel a tiny bit guilty for not working late.

TREAT IT LIKE A PROJECT

So with all that blocking of time, how do you get stuff done?

> Treat your workday and tasks as a project.
> Prioritize, scope, focus, timebox. Don't idle at
> work, instead focus and spend your idle time on
> the things you care about.

We need to treat our work tasks like projects. We need to deliberately manage them instead of just keep going until we will be done at some undefined point in the future, with an undefined amount of time and effort invested to get there.

Start your project now, and don't procrastinate it, even if the start scares you. Every journey starts with the first step.

Avoid unnecessary rework. Put your best foot forward, and get it right the first time. If you don't, learn what was missing and make super–sure you will get it right the next time you have a similar problem to solve. Nothing eats more time and energy (and is more frustrating) than repeated rework and fixing of the same issues.

Timebox how much time you spend on something (after all you want to free up time for the passions we talked about above). Prioritize what needs to get done versus what only seems urgent or important. If the work is too much, see if you can scope it down without harming the overall outcome. Can you remove unnecessary 'bells and whistles'? Timebox, and then be extremely focused in that time–box to deliver your best work most efficiently. Treat it like an engineering 'dev spike.' When you hit the end of your timebox, stop. You need to train yourself to take your focus times serious.

If it's still too much, it's ok to say 'no' to things. Just know and be clear why you say 'no' and what trade-offs you're making. Communicate the reasons and trade-offs. Communicate them early. It's ok not to be able to tackle something if everyone knows about it and has enough time to come up with a mitigation plan (even better if you can propose a mitigation plan yourself). It's not ok to let something slip past the deadline and then announce that you didn't have time.

Be focused, cut out the slack. Rather than idling at work, double down, be your most focused self and then spend your freed-up time on the things you care about at work and at home.

MAKING DAISY CHAINS TAKES MY MIND OFF

We need to listen more to our kids; they are the true teachers.

I was making daisy chains with our daughter today – actually she taught me how to make daisy chains. Seeing her work quietly, I asked her what was going through her mind.

Her answer was worthy of a Zen master:

I don't think anything when I make daisy chains. Making daisy chains takes my mind off.

Had I asked the same question to an adult, I would have gotten a long list of unrelated thoughts back.

There's a lot to learn from our daughter.

- Be in the moment. Focus on what you're doing.
- Don't worry about other things while you're doing what you like.
- Find pleasure and passion in the things you're doing right now.

Watch your kids closely; there's a lot we can learn from them!

SMALL CHANGES CAN HAVE HUGE IMPACT

I am not obsessed with my weight. To me, weight is just one input to an overall healthy life and lifestyle. However, I noticed that I had gained almost 15 pounds over the last half–year without really knowing why. That disturbed and frustrated me, to be honest.

I did make a plan to do more sports but couldn't follow through to the extent that I wished due to work demands. I didn't increase my workout frequency at all. So I decided to accept the gain for now and tackle it in a few months when work demands have calmed down a little bit.

Surprisingly, over the last few weeks, I noticed that my weight had dropped back down ten pounds. I didn't focus on anything specific to get there. I didn't even know what caused it. So I went on a little inventory of changes that I had made to my rhythms and habits lately:

- I stopped drinking my one or two glasses of wine with dinner in the evening to have a better sleep
- I stopped drinking a protein shake in the morning and a few lattes throughout the day because milk left me with a 'slimy' feeling which I wanted to reduce
- I wanted to leverage the quiet morning hours at work and thus skipped reading the news in the morning, instead going straight

to the shower, which also meant I wouldn't eat the four pieces of chocolate while checking for news

Those are the only lifestyle changes I can think of, yet they made me get back towards my optimal weight without explicitly trying.

Small changes do have an outsized impact!

Don't try to make big swoops of dramatic changes to your life. They are hard. Instead chip away on the small things and allow them to add up.

IF YOU MAKE A MISTAKE KEEP GOING

W hat's the difference between a beginner making a mistake and a master making the same mistake?

The beginner will notice the mistake, stop, blame himself for making the stupid mistake and maybe even stop altogether for the day in frustration. He might contemplate for a long while, why this mistake has happened, and how embarrassing the situation was.

The master accepts the situation and keeps going without a blink. Later, when there is time, she will reflect on what led to the mistake and how she might be able to prevent it in the future. She will practice the situation and be prepared to deal with it the next time it might occur. She will not waste energy to dwell in self–blame or pity.

I once saw this mindset live in the perfect demonstration. Tsuguo Sakumoto, a 9th-degree black belt and the leader of Ryuei–Ryu karate, demonstrated a Kama kata. Kama are Okinawan sickles. They have razor-sharp blades, and the kata (form) consists of lightning-fast movements swirling two Kamas through the air at the same time.

Master Sakumoto made a mistake while demonstrating this kata to a crowd of about a hundred people, all highly ranked karatekas. One of the blades came in contact with the handle of the other. It cut right through the wood and made the other blade fly high through the air. Master Sakumoto was lucky that he hadn't cut off some fingers.

This was a scary moment, a pretty bad mistake, and could have been embarrassing. Other athletes might have gone in frustration and maybe thrown their tennis rack on the ground, storming out of the court. Not the karate master. He kept going as if nothing had happened. Not a moment of hesitation, not a blink, not a flinch. He was a hundred percent committed and finished the form. After that, he bowed, went, picked up the other blade, and was ready for questions from the audience.

Be in the moment. Finish what you have started. Don't get thrown off by what you didn't expect. Don't dwell in analysis and get stuck in something that has already happened and which you can't influence anymore. Think about it when you have time and then move on.

When you make a mistake in your practice, don't miss a beat. Realize and acknowledge what has happened. Decide if you need to adjust and move on in the same instance. Don't let it throw you off.

The same is true for life. When you hit a bump in the road, you need to keep going. Practice this mindset in martial arts. Make it your second nature and then make sure you apply the same mindset in your daily life.

DON'T SABOTAGE YOUR WINS

CONSTANT DROPPING WEARS AWAY A STONE

A nd paper cuts can kill you...

Most people are focused on the big, challenging, and shiny projects, and that's important. However, while we're driving the big blocks and highly visible deliverables, we <u>must not drop the ball</u> on the more mundane promises we have made (e.g., project updates, the task we prom-

ised our co-worker, newsletter updates, that email from our boss,... – you name it).

> Don't undermine your big wins by being sloppy on the small and mundane tasks.

THE PROBLEM WITH (MANY) LITTLE MISSES

We all miss something every now and then. That's normal and ok. The problem arises, when it happens repeatedly so that people start assuming you will miss a promise with a high–enough probability. They will lose trust in you, and your reputation will erode. Once it looks like a pattern, you have a problem that you must solve.

Bringing in the big wins and celebrations is fantastic! Be proud of it! Others will see them and recognize you for the achievement.

However, if there are small misses sprinkled throughout the big wins, people will remember the constant small signal much more than the sporadic big signal. What would you remember more, if I brought you a nice hot latte every morning or a $100 bill once a month? No, sorry, I won't do either, it's just a thought experiment.

Visibility is in the small things. If they don't create confidence, we have a problem. Little mistakes add up and can neutralize all the good stuff you worked so hard for.

In our roles as managers, coaches, or parents, we all know the situation. We want the best for our employees, coachees, and kids. We want them to stack up wins. As we watch them over the weeks we all too often go: "Nice, nice, nice – oh shit, WHY did they do this?" Then we start back from square one.

TACTICS TO AVOID MISSES

On the highest level, there are three key strategies to avoid creating a pattern of little misses:

Accountability: Track your promises

This is the most basic and simplest one. If you sign up for an action item, write it down right away. Block time in your calendar. If you can't do it, say 'no' right away (read that Friday musing). No excuses after that.

Quality: Slow down and double–check

Don't just try to get rid of an annoying task. Chances are you will miss a key point, or your numbers or answer won't make sense. Usually, one of two things will happen as a result: either you will look like you don't know what you're doing, or an escalation will happen further down the road. You don't need either.

Comprehensiveness: Ask yourself, "What am I missing?"

The most frustrating thing for a (senior) leader is to have a question or count on a deliverable and then getting something that doesn't solve the actual problem or answer the core question. Now the leader has to spend time following up and chasing down what you need. Prevent that from happening. As yourself what you're missing and what the logical next question would be.

A WORD ABOUT MANAGING SENIOR LEADERS

Senior leaders have to fight a hundred fires at any given time. They need to continually switch context between vastly different problem spaces. In meetings that is every 30 mins, in their inbox, it is from email to email (i.e., within seconds). They don't have all the details you have, and they might have forgotten a detail you shared a few weeks ago. They need to compartmentalize problems, quickly switch their thinking, recreate the full context of a new problem, get issues solved on the spot, and move on. Hundred times a day.

If they are not super-efficient with getting into a new context, understanding the problem and proposed solution on the spot and moving on, they will drown. Because of that, they usually have a very allergic reaction to anything that lacks context, is not thought through, doesn't add up or leaves key questions open. Unless specifically booked, they don't have time to brainstorm with you.

Understanding these constraints, there are critical things to do when responding to senior leaders:

- **Provide context** – Don't make them have to follow–up with questions to understand what you mean.
- **Be concise and crisp** – Don't make them have to search the answers to their concern in vast deserts of random data and words.
- **Close all loops** (or at least provide timelines for when they will be closed) – Don't make them continue keeping the topic on their worry list.
- **Get it done in your first reply** – Don't make them have to continue context switch in an email brainstorming conversation over days.
- **Double–check** – Put yourself in the shoes of the recipient. Go over your answer and pretend not to have the context. Does it still make sense? Does everything add up?

Understand the intent

To achieve the above qualities in your response, specifically 'getting it done in your fist reply,' it is critical to not just answer the question at face value but to understand the intent.

Don't just answer the immediate question or drop the data. Understand the intent! Ask yourself: *"What is the requestor trying to achieve?"*.

Once you understand the intent, what the requestor wants to achieve, you get a better sense of what additional information or context they might need. What further questions were not asked but are required to accomplish that intent? Provide the answers proactively!

Now make it consumable. Structure the data such that it serves the question and the underlying intent, and the flow is easy to follow and understand.

HERE'S AN ACTION FOR YOU

Spend a minute to reflect:

- What action items and promises to others did you miss the last two weeks?
- How many email threads with leadership did you have that required multiple inquiries and follow-ups from the leader?
- How often was the quality of content not where it should have been for a review because you haven't thought it through deeply enough?

What can you do to avoid and change that in the future?

THE IMPORTANCE OF PRESENTATION AND ATTENTION TO DETAILS

Presentation and attention to details are about making your ideas and content more impactful after you have covered all the bases. It's an 'and' not an 'either/or.' It's about 'Insisting on highest standards' all the way through.

Not form over function but form <u>and</u> function.

DESIGN MATTERS AND ATTENTION TO DETAILS MATTERS

Steve Jobs famously turned around Apple by obsessing on details – even those that aren't visible to customers, like the visual clarity of the physical layout of the components in an iPhone, or the visual design and cleanliness of Apple's factory floors.

Should that matter? Why isn't function the only thing we should care about? Do we really need to refine the presentation of our content once the facts are there? YES!

Details matter. Presentation matters. Fit and finish matters.

Think about your own experiences. You (probably) like Apple products. Why? You could use any other computer/phone and would be able to do the same things: write documents, make calls, catch up on stuff. However, you don't, you find pleasure in things that are well crafted and where attention to details has been amply paid.

You likely had much more fun with your phone when it was new and without scratches. Why? It still fulfills the same functionality. Why should you care about it no longer being flawless in every aspect of its appearance?

How would you think if someone scratched your new car? It still drives just the same. Will it matter to you?

How about a precious gift for your loved ones? Would you wrap it in ugly, crappy and crumbled paper?

EVERYTHING IS A SELL. EVERYTHING IS A PRESENTATION

Ok, here is where I'm going with this:

> Everything is a sell, even if you sell primarily through data (function), you still have to sell.

All too often, I see people spending much time in thinking through problems, collecting data, working hard on the details – and then dropping the ball on presentation.

Supposedly small things destroy the overall impression that your content makes: hastily copy–pasted emails that are painful to read, documents where formatting of lists, paragraph alignment or spacing changes from paragraph to paragraph, inconsistent bolding, Xs and Ys that are forgotten in the text (do a simple search!), appendices that were not updated, supporting data that doesn't pass a simple sniff–test…

If you don't give your content that last final touch, you give away a significant part of the impact that your hard work could have. Doing a final check on 'design' and 'details' is probably the best bang for the buck you can get on any document that you have worked on for several hours. Invest that time!

Word has grammar checkers, go to full–page view to check alignments, search for Xs and Ys, check every appendix and make sure it received some love. Read your document or presentation one more time as if you didn't know it. Better even, ask someone else to read it – not for the content but the presentation.

Don't undersell your work. It's not only the data but also the presentation. Even if people tell you that it doesn't matter, subconsciously it makes a huge difference. Would you rather get the scratched phone handed down or the same model that's sparkly new?

Make it readable, engaging, and make it look like you care. What you do matters, make it count! Have pride in your work and show that pride!

Obsession for detail differentiates Great from just Ok.

Last not least, you are also sending a message to the reviewer: "This is good enough for you; I don't care enough to make it nicer/clearer." Sometimes you might do that consciously and strategically, but I assume in most cases, you didn't have that intention.

Bring your work over the finish line and make it matter!

DEVELOP AN ACCOUNTABILITY MINDSET AND CULTURE

High performing teams trust each other. Like raising an orchid, building trust requires a lot of attention and dedication to nurture, but it can be broken by a single mistake.

If you cannot trust your teammates, morale will go down. If you cannot trust your manager,

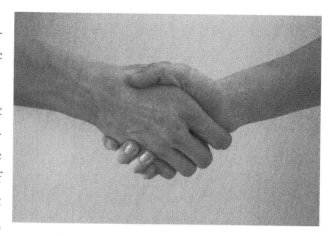

you will hate to go to work. If you cannot trust your employee, you will avoid giving them critical work.

ACCOUNTABILITY MATTERS

Accountability is one of the significant inputs to trust. Can you depend on your coworker's deliverable to be ready in time and quality when you need it? Or do you need to chase them down, or worst case have to fix issues yourself in the last minute?

Decide if you commit, but once you do it, do it wholeheartedly.

Accountability does not mean that you have to say yes to everything. However, once you do, make it a personal promise. Make it a matter of personal pride and values to come through on your promises.

ASKING FOR HELP – BE SPECIFIC

Be specific when you ask someone for help. Don't make ambiguous statements like "Someone should do X." No one will feel responsible. In first responder training, they teach you to point to a person and tell them precisely what to do. Otherwise no one will hear you.

> Ask directly, explaining the 'why': "To achieve X, can you do Y by Z?"

AGREEING TO HELP – TREAT IT AS A PERSONAL PROMISE

When you are asked to help, you don't have to say 'yes.' You don't have to agree to the timeline right away. It's ok to explain tradeoffs if you take on that new task. It's ok to ask what drives the deadline and offer a different date that you can make. Ask questions, understand reason and priority, be clear what you can do by when before you commit.

Once you commit, you commit. It's not ok to pay lip service and then let the other person hang. It's not a badge of honor to miss a promise because you were "too busy."

You need to make a personal promise or say 'no.' Right there and then. Don't leave it ambiguous, hoping a miracle happens along the way or everyone will forget.

> When you do commit and confirm, be specific: "I will do X by Y."

After you committed, block time in your calendar right away. Treat your commitment as a personal promise. Delivering against your commitment will not only impact how you are viewed in the team; it also subconsciously reflects on how you perceive your own integrity.

In many ways, the worst impact one has by not delivering on promises is on oneself.

NOT EVERYTHING IS AS URGENT AS IT APPEARS

A critical part of being accountable and delivering against your commitments (promises!) is to actually have the bandwidth for them, in other words, to not overcommit.

We already talked about how it is ok – actually expected – to say 'no' when needed. What we didn't talk about yet are timelines (or 'deadlines' to make it even scarier sounding).

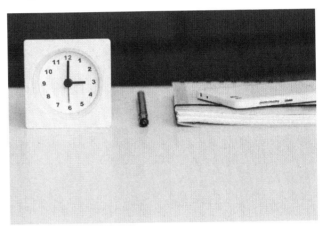

Not everything is as urgent as it might appear at first glance.

CLARIFY EXPECTATIONS

Not everything that comes from your leadership comes with a "drop everything else and do this right now" expectation. In most cases, leaders just want to know when they can expect an answer and have the confidence that they don't need to spend their energy to track that deliverable for you.

Don't assume. Clarify and verify.

If a request came in without a timeline or clarification on urgency, don't assume. Just ask: "Hey, when do you need this by?"

No decent leader will hold it against you if you ask, "By when do you need this?" I'm pretty sure for most leaders this will register as a plus point (if it doesn't it's time to look for a different leader).

What leaders want to know is whether you commit to providing the answer and by when. They want to be confident that you will do it and that they don't have to worry about it. They will tell you if a timeline is not flexible and why.

As an employee, train your leader to provide that information with her requests in the future. However, also make extra-sure that you are managing yourself against that timeline! It is super frustrating as a leader if you need to keep your own reminders on everything you need because you cannot rely on open loops to be closed without your constant follow-up.

UNDERSTAND TIMELINES

Not everything needs to happen right now. Very few things are truly urgent, although many are perceived or presented as urgent or initially appear non-negotiable.

Unfortunately, corporate culture has developed many bad habits to try to compensate for low accountability:

- Setting deadlines way ahead of time to build in a buffer
- Setting short deadlines so that people do it right now and don't get distracted
- Setting deadlines just because that's what you do

- And the worst: setting a short deadline because something was sitting idle on your own desk for too long and now it's really time to make progress

---

Understand the true urgency and timeline. Offer a plan to get there. Make sure you hit that plan.

Feel empowered to understand and validate urgency and tight deadlines. Ask for when a task is truly due. If it requires you to drop other things, understand what drives the urgency and what breaks if the deadline is missed.

If you think a deadline has a 'safety buffer' built in, ask for the real deadline. However, once you get the real deadline, you must make sure that you will be ready by that time. Otherwise, you teach your partners to add additional buffers to manage in the future to work around your tardiness and unreliability.

If a deadline is infeasible, check your calendar and priorities and see when you can make it. Offer that alternative plan and check for agreement. If pushed, be clear what you will have to sacrifice to make that timeline.

In most cases, you will find that a deadline is negotiable.

HOW TO DEVELOP AND SELL A STRATEGY

S trategic planning is the holy grail of leadership. Or is it?

Let's talk about mental models for strategic planning (e.g., three-year plans, business strategies) and also how to best communicate the outcomes – the famous 'evangelizing.'

Strategic planning is all about setting the <u>right priorities</u> to have the most significant impact on <u>desired outcomes</u>. Strategic planning is setting the goal post; tactical execution is getting there (it took me about ten years of my professional career to truly understand that – I can be a slow learner).

Strategic planning is – or should be – working backwards. The question should not be "what can I do next" but "where do I need to be three years from now." With that, it always starts with getting clarity on the end state, the goals and the big problems to solve.

Always start with the 'why". What do you want to achieve and why does it matter? Once you know the destination and purpose you can chart your path to get there.

WHERE DO YOU NEED TO BE IN THREE YEARS?

What are the goals (even better: what is THE goal)?

Identify the goals that you need to achieve. How can you measure whether you make progress against those goals?

Understand why they matter and how they might be correlated (positively or negatively) to each other.

What have you learned? What are your fundamental insights?

Goals are great metrics for progress, but there might also be significant fundamental or structural issues that need to be solved but are not immediately apparent from looking at the goals.

It's good practice to reflect on what you have learned since the last strategic planning. Did new fundamental problems or constraints present themselves that can have a material impact on your ability to achieve the goals? Did new opportunities present themselves that weren't obvious the last time?

Think backwards, not forward!

Don't constrain yourself by what you know and have (e.g., current capabilities, existing funding, roadmaps, and team structures).

Define where you need to be. Figure out how to get there in the next step.

"If all you have is a hammer, everything looks like a nail." – Forget that you have a hammer for a moment, think about what you need to do and only then about what tool you might have to acquire.

What are your big levers?

Now that you know your goals, problems, and opportunities – how can you have the most impact on those? What are your biggest levers?

Brainstorm

Make a list of all the things (the means to an end) that will help you to move towards the end state you want to achieve in 3 years.

Again, don't limit yourself by the current structure or what tech pieces you have. Think about what you need to move the goal, solve the problem, or seize the opportunity.

Force yourself (!) to not just think about thinks you 'could do' but focus on what spefically will move the priorities you defined previously.

Prioritize

You cannot do everything you came up with in your brainstorming. You need to decide what to do first, what to focus on. No peanut–buttering.

What are the few things that will have an outsized impact on your ability to achieve the desired end state?

Identify the biggest levers. Look at the outcome/impact, but also the cost/feasibility (i.e., what's the Return of Investment, the ROI, of an idea). Make a sorted list of your biggest levers, their impact, and their cost. Once you have that list, you and your leadership can draw the line wherever you think the right ROI tradeoff is for investments.

Solidify your case

Get data. Make sure your initial assumptions are correct, and the ROI story holds water.

Understand more details and make sure the idea is still feasible.

Start making a worry list or risk tracker (i.e., what could go wrong?) and burn it down. This process will not end until your final project is shipped. Having a risk tracker or worry list is generally a good practice to avoid surprises.

SELL YOUR STORY!

By now, you have put a LOT of thinking into your proposal. Be mindful that no one else has any comparable context or level of detail. You will need to catch up readers wholly and quickly.

The best way to do that is to recreate your thought process for them in your storytelling. Here's a story flow that works.

Start with the goals

What do you want to achieve? What are your measurable priorities?

Why do they matter? Why these and not others?

Proper framing

What is the environment you are operating in? What have you learned (e.g., problems, opportunities)?

What assumptions about the future are you making that further inform your plans and thinking? What constraints do you need to work with?

What multipliers can you leverage?

Prioritization

Why did you pick the things you picked? What did you identify as the most significant levers and why (ROI)?

What did you push below the line and why (that's an excellent appendix to have, especially when leaders are looking for additional projects to fund)? What are the most painful tradeoffs, and what would it take to bring them back in?

This part is the 'money piece,' you either get decision makers on board because they can follow your reasoning or you lose them because they cannot recreate what prioritization and tradeoffs you made.

Get tactical

Start giving a preview of how you will deploy your levers.

This is where reality kicks in.

From your current state, what are the next steps? What are rough timelines on how you would go about solving your problems as well as building and deploying your solutions?

What are the big questions you need to answers? Is there anything you need from leadership (play this card carefully and deliberately)?

GO DO IT!

You have a plan. You have approval. Go Execute!

MAKE YOUR VOICE HEARD

I have to confess: I'm an introvert. Big time.

I'm also a successful evangelist, company spokesperson, people manager, and leader amongst extroverts. So how does that work? You guessed wrong; the answer is not schizophrenia.

Let's first look a little closer to what it means to be an introvert. If you are an extro-vert, you proba-

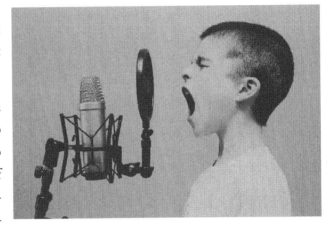

bly want to stop reading now; this is secret stuff (chances are you're already bored anyway). If you are an introvert, this is for you!

First of all, there's a broad misconception that introversion/extraversion describes what you CAN do. It does NOT! It's merely an expression of your natural subconscious preference. It explains where you pull your energy from. Let me repeat: introversion/extroversion does NOT limit what you CAN do! Moreover, introversion comes with many superpow-ers.

YOUR STRENGTHS

Having a preference for introversion usually means that you tend to think before you speak (versus forming your thoughts by conversing with others). By the way, I'm not saying that extroverts don't think, their thought process just tends to work more through expression, exchange, and refinement of thoughts while they discuss.

You also tend to think deeply about things and consider all details and implications. You can do this because you don't get distracted in your thought process by competing ideas from others, while you are still forming your own opinion.

Both are superpowers if used correctly. They can also be severe limitations if not appropriately managed.

YOUR WEAKNESS

Because you like to think deeply about things before sharing, there's a considerable risk that you will repeatedly come up with brilliant solutions only to find out that 'the train has already left the station'.

Most of us introverts think that we can't share a plan until we have it nailed 100%. That's wrong. Having 80% is excellent! Having even only 60% to get a conversation started and begin enrolling everyone else is just fine too. Remember, the extroverts in your team need to see the plan evolving through discussion or they are likely to reject it and start a verbal thought process from scratch (there goes your brilliant plan).

Trying to get everything nailed down 100% will also make many of us fearful of speaking up in larger groups or even giving presentations at meetings or events. Drop that fear. In fact, introverts are fantastic speakers! Accept that you have only mastered 80% of your area of expertise. Guess what, everyone else likely only has a shallow 40% or so – that's the reason why you were asked to be the speaker in the first place.

The last significant weakness is that most introverts believe that others will actively look for and naturally discover their greatness. Bad news: that won't happen. There's a career problem here. The good news is: We can fix it.

HOW YOU CAN SHINE (MORE)

So what do we do to become even (more) impactful? Let's go from easy to hard (at least that was my personal experience).

Social media

Good news is you're a natural for this.

Having introvert preferences, you likely spend time reading, researching, and thinking. You have precious thoughts, share them! You also tend to get to the point quickly, to be concise and to leave out all the fluff. Readers love that.

Start engaging, start re-sharing, and commenting. Then get into expressing and sharing your genuine thoughts. Social media is a powerful way of sharing your thoughts and networking broadly, without all that small talk stuff (yikes!). It empowers you to consistently build up and hone your personal brand.

It's easy and natural for you. Just do it; don't be lazy.

Presentations and events

You probably have already noticed that speaking isn't hard for you either, once you choose to do it (and once you overcome your initial fears).

Your biggest concern typically is whether what you have to say is worth sharing. Drop that. You're the expert, that's why someone chose you as the speaker. You might not know everything, but you do know so much more than your audience. Go for it, share what you know!

People will perceive you as a great speaker for the same reasons that they will like your social media writing. You don't talk for talking's sake. You also don't think as you speak, instead, you have a clearly thought out map in your mind which you will follow and unfold together with your audience. In short, you don't waste their time.

You are detail focused, which can be a little lengthy at times. Be conscious of this and find the right balance not to bore and lose your audience.

Getting some solid speaker training is an excellent advice for everyone. If you get an opportunity to present, go for it!

Meetings and decision–making

I already touched on an introvert's tendency to have everything nailed down and polished 100% before showing it to the broader world. Scratch that approach right now and here. Unless everyone around you is an introvert too, it's a recipe for failure.

Share early, share broadly, share frequently. If you have it 40% down, you're ready to get thoughts and feedbacks towards the direction in your plan. When you have it 60% down, it's time to evangelize everyone on your plan and get active buy-in. When you're at 80%, ship it! You can still drive it to 100% if your idea turns out to become a huge success and is being widely implemented. Yes, I'm serious about this!

When sharing and evangelizing your plan to a new set of peers, sometimes it's more effective to pretend you don't have a grand master plan yet (even if you do) and instead let the new folks come to the same conclusions that you reached earlier. Gently guide the discussion so that the team can get to the same place where you are. That's not always the right strategy. Often you are just meant to present what the plan is. However, sometimes it works wonders to get folks on board quicker. "Here's the problem. Here's the data. Here are some thoughts we heard. What do you think? Ah great, how about this?" – Sold.

In meetings, make yourself heard. Yes, this might sound cruel, but you have to speak up. In brainstorming sessions go first, so you don't have to fight for the loudest voice once everyone else chimes in. Then go again last, to make the point that turns everything around and sticks in people's minds. You will notice that often, more extrovert groups will need some time for 'vocal thinking' before they are ready to listen to and consider your well thought through conclusions.

Promote yourself

If you're like me, this is the hardest one and the one that we need to manage most consciously. You don't like to talk about the things you achieved. Those should be obvious right!?

Celebrating the success of others or writing down accomplishments of folks in my team comes naturally to me. I can effortlessly talk all day about the great things my direct reports accomplish every day. Writing my own performance review, résumé or LinkedIn profile is the hardest thing ever.

There is a saying in Germany that luckily, one of my colleagues told me early in my days with Microsoft: "Do good things and talk about them!" I wish I could remember who gave me that advice; it was the best career advice ever (for an introvert – if there are still some extroverts around reading this, please DON'T try to talk more about your achievements)!

Don't force it though, or you will feel eternally bad and corrupted. Find your way that feels authentic and doesn't violate your values. If you're a manager, it's easier, talk about the great stuff your team achieved. If you're an individual contributor, talk about the progress that your project team has made or talk about how you learned that your customers used your work to become more productive. If you're working all alone in your cubicle, update your LinkedIn profile and find a better job.

If you don't like talking about how great you are, shift your focus, and share how customers, partners, or team members were able to be more successful because of what you did. Don't forget to call out how what you contributed to that fantastic outcome. Start by giving credit but don't understate your contributions.

FINAL THOUGHT

> "I became a martial artist in spite of my limitations."
> Bruce Lee

Best advice ever. Perceived limitations (or boxes we put ourselves into) don't limit what we can do – our mental model does. Understand your ~~limitations~~ preferences and turn them into an advantage!

BECOME A BETTER LEADER

Being a leader should mean that you maintain a learning mindset and continuously aspire to improve and grow. Being a leader is (or at least should be) a journey, not a destination.

There's TONS of fantastic advice out there on what

leaders should do. The flip side of this is that it's easy to get overwhelmed by all the things you are supposed to do.

I like to focus on a few things at a time – usually the power of three works for me. I can keep up to three things in my head. After that, things will get messy and messed up. Here are the three things I focus on for growing my team, as well as the three things for growing myself. They are quite powerful and work beautifully for me.

> You are here to help your team find Purpose, Mastery and Autonomy. Support their growth, and never forget that YOUR learning as a leader will never end.

GROW YOUR TEAM

Motivation has always been a big topic in leadership. It's been established for a while that money alone doesn't do the trick. Everyone wants to get a decent paycheck for what they do, but that alone won't keep folks motivated.

A coworker recently pointed me to a TED talk by Dan Pink that resonated with me. Dan explains that there are three major components that create or destroy job satisfaction and motivation. I won't do Dan justice with my words, and you should listen to the TED talk, but here are my three personal homework assignments from his talk.

Provide purpose

We spend a LOT of time at work. We want that time to count for something. Understanding the purpose of what we do is very important (if you can't find purpose in what you do, look for another job).

As a leader, that means that just delegating work is not enough. You need to engage people by explaining the 'why' and the broader picture. They need to understand why the work that they do is important. They need to see how it fits into the broader mission of the organization.

Along the same lines: praising results is essential. That acknowledgment or 'thank you' becomes even more potent if you clearly explain how these achievements helped advance a higher goal for the organization.

Give autonomy

Work sucks if you aren't empowered to make decisions. It also sucks if you have to explain your decisions to everyone again and again. In this case, in reality, you actually don't make the decision; you instead repeatedly have to ask for re-approval from everyone.

For many leaders, this is a tough one. We usually think that we are so much smarter. That's why we became leaders in the first place, right? Wrong!

However often we have more experience because we've been in the area longer. We are also regularly exposed to a broader picture of what's going on in the organization. Having that experience and more comprehensive view is incredible if it is used for coaching. It becomes destructive if it leads to micromanaging.

Let go of doing things by yourself or being ultra–prescriptive. Let go of making the decisions for your team members. Instead, provide the right data and context. Guide your team in developing the best decision framework. Empower your team members. Ask questions to understand better the solutions your team proposed. Moreover, let them make the decisions – you can always jump in if they seem to head in a terribly wrong direction.

Of course, there is a spectrum for this. If someone is new to a problem space, he will need more guidance. If someone is well versed in an area, she will want less direction. Situational Leadership II is a great framework to find the right level of management.

Nurture mastery

We all want to be great at what we do. Moreover, if we aren't yet, we want to learn how to become great. Mastery of an area is a fantastic feeling!

Mastery requires trying and learning. As a leader, you need to create the right balance between freedom to experiment and gentle guidance. People need to try things. They have to be allowed to make mistakes to learn. They also crave for just enough direction to be successful, while not getting too frustrated in the process.

This is where leaders need to focus on being great coaches and mentors rather than mere managers. We need to force ourselves to stay away from doing things ourselves or prescribing the 'right' solution because we think that would lead to quicker results. We must stay away from managing every detail and instead give feedback along the way, while we let the team explore possible solutions.

Honestly, I'm still failing at this one too often. The important thing is that I'm now conscious of the challenge, and I'm working on myself.

There's also an exception to the rule: sometimes you have to step in and take over because there is an urgent deadline. In those cases, there is no time for trying and learning; things need to get done right NOW. If you let your team know why you step in for this particular case, it will be much less harmful for team motivation. Hopefully, this is the exception, not the rule in your team.

GROW YOURSELF

Yes, you are a leader, and most of what you achieve gets done by your team and not yourself. Leading and growing your team is your top priority. However, that doesn't relieve you from taking a hard look at how you perform individually.

I got inspired to this section by a post from Jeff Weiner talking about the three qualities in people he most enjoys working with.

Again I won't do the breadth and depth of the original post justice, so please jump over there and read it for yourself. Below are the three homework assignments I took away for myself.

Dream big

I'm a 'getting things done' person. That can sometimes mean that I focus too much on resolving tactical issues and roadblocks because I want to get them out of the way as quickly as possible. The problem is that there are always some tactical issues that will distract you from the bigger picture.

If you don't dream big, you won't accomplish anything meaningful. Mediocrity will be your world, not greatness.

As with everything else, awareness and consciousness already get you 80% down the way to the solution. If you are a 'go–doer,' block time to dream big. Reserve time, where you will not allow yourself to 'fix stuff.' Look at the big picture and think about the impossible. Then make a plan for how to get there!

I make it a point to spend time thinking about the bigger picture and bigger aspirations. I put a recurring time blocker on my calendar.

Get things done

This one comes naturally to me.

I write everything on a 'to-do' list. Once it's on my 'to-do' list, I don't have to remember it anymore, and my mind frees up to think about more interesting questions.

My 'to-do' list is always long, but I hate having a long list. That's a great motivator to get things done, one by one. Sort your list by priorities. Then work your way from the top towards the bottom. Finish as much as you can achieve in the allotted time. Focus on finishing. Instead, start fewer things, but complete the ones you started. Moreover, be ok if you got less done, than you had planned (hoped). Life happens. You're good as long as you kept the focus on the most important things and made progress on those.

From time to time, you should also look at your low priorities. Most of them will turn out to not be as important anymore. Remove them from the list.

Instead of worrying about all the things that need to be done, just write them down, prioritize them and get on it.

Be great to work with

I think this one was 'fun to work with' in Jeff's post. I'm a German and as such inherently not fun(ny), so I changed this one a little bit.

To me, the critical quality is to be great to work with (not necessarily fun). Greatness can have multiple aspects. It can mean that you are a fun person. It can also mean that you are a great mentor, a valuable resource for your coworkers, a supportive person, or a critical sounding board to bounce ideas off.

Find what makes you great to work with and hone that skill. I cannot help you with this one; you have to find your superpowers and build on what makes you unique. Bonus points if you also critically explore, what makes you suck and then work extra hard to get rid of those behaviors.

Finally, get folks (and yourself) out of their comfort zone. **That's when amazing things will happen!**

SINGLE THREADED LEADERSHIP AT AMAZON

Single Threaded Leaders (STLs) are core to Amazon's leadership philosophy. We are all STLs for one thing or another. However, what does that mean?

A STL is the one person who owns success or failure of a given initiative, project, or goal. They are the decision maker or the one who is responsible for driving decisions. They are the single point of contact and the one who answers for the project. The STL is the one who  doesn't have excuses for not raising an issue, driving a decision, and moving the project forward.

Less polite descriptions used in other companies are 'butt on the line' or 'throat to choke.' I do NOT think that's the right way to think about it though!

HOW TO BE SUCCESSFUL AS A STL

We all strive to be effective leaders; in Amazon-speak strong STLs. So what makes a strong STL?

IT STARTS WITH OWNERSHIP

Being a STL means that you OWN the projects you were given responsibility for (better even: you took responsibility for). It also means that you feel **fully responsible** for the success of that project. There is no one else to point a finger to or to blame.

However, it **does not** mean that you need to fix or do everything yourself. Far from that!

Ownership doesn't mean that you need to do everything yourself. It does mean that you need to make sure the right things are happening, and the right people know about status changes early on. Delegate and orchestrate!

Ownership means that you own the progress, understand when things go sideways, and either put the right fixes in place to correct course or escalate quickly if problems/fixes are beyond your control. You don't need to be afraid if things don't always go the way as initially planned. However, you should feel bad if things go sideways, and you didn't try proper actions and escalations.

COME WITH A SOLUTION

When things go sideways, and a fix is beyond your scope of control, you need to escalate up **quickly**. Speed matters. There are few things a manager hates more than being surprised at a time when they are out of options to help you out.

How do you escalate if you need help? Come with a solution!

> Followers come with a problem; leaders come
> with a solution.

Present the problem, give a short explanation on the root cause that got you there, and then offer a solution proposal. Ideally, also explain the alternatives and why you picked that specific proposal (what were the pros and cons of the other options?).

Explain how far you were able to push within your scope of influence, what you tried, and what specific help you now need from your leader. Help them understand the tradeoffs that need to be made. Be clear what specific help you need or what action you are taking for which you need backup from your leader.

Do **not** only come with a problem or open-ended question. Your leader will most likely jump on the opportunity to solve it for you, but that will harm your authority as STL and also deprives you of the sense of control over your project.

A QUICK GLIMPSE INTO THE MIND OF YOUR LEADERS

Leaders like to problem-solve. That's how they grew up, how they became leaders. However, as a leader, the ultimate goal is to grow their impact by delegating spheres of problem ownership and knowing they will get solved locally as much as possible (and without needing to keep track of progress).

So when presented with an open-ended question or problem, a leader will jump into solving it for you (unless they are an outstanding leader, in which case they will try hard to hold themselves back). However, after your meeting they will have that nagging question in their mind: 'why did I have to solve this, what did I do wrong?' Help your leader to not wrangle with that question!

Help your leader to scale to the next level by showing them that you own your space at the next level.

WHAT MAKES A GREAT STL?

Know that you are empowered. Don't just say it, know it, feel it!
Feel responsible for the end to end! Fully.
Own driving the solution, or if you can't, own having a solution and asking for proper help.
Escalate when you exhausted your options or ideas or spent too much time trying – understand the point when you need to go up.

CONFIDENCE ESTABLISHES AUTHORITY

Most of us are working in an environment and culture in which we (luckily!) cannot just demand someone to follow our orders. We're not McDonald's. We are all working with highly skilled and experienced professionals who will only follow us if we earn their trust and gain authority through our actions, not hierarchy. I would not want it any other way!

So, how do you gain authority as a leader in your org and with partners?

COMPETENCY

Step one is to have your act together. You need to know what you know and what you don't. Don't pretend you know something, only to then be called out on your gaps. Don't makeup stuff if you want to be trusted and followed.

Of course, you will want to close the gap on the things that you don't know as quickly as possible. Ask lots of questions, learn, reflect, understand.

Learning and deeply understanding your space is the 101, so I will not spend any further time on this. I wanted to call it out though since authority without understanding isn't sustainable in our space.

BE BOLD, ACCEPT THE RISK TO FAIL

As a leader, you are expected to make tough calls and bold decisions. You cannot do that if you are afraid of risk or scared of failing. Also, if you don't make bold calls, people will not follow you because quite frankly you are not leading.

> As a leader, you cannot play it safe. Take calculated risks but take risks. Free your mind by allowing yourself the option to fail.

When I look back at my different leadership roles, I can see a clear pattern of being most impactful as a leader when I had the least concern about what I could potentially lose. I was bold, took the right risks, and set unambiguous direction when I wasn't scared about failing or losing something. I was lame when I was so concerned about a particular personal outcome or gain, that I tried to avoid anything that could put that outcome at risk.

The good news is that the loss avoidance mindset is a question of your perspective, and subsequently, you are in control to change it. It is the human default though, which means you need to put in serious energy to change it.

Leadership means making bold decisions and taking calculated risks. As a leader, you need to bring (disruptive) energy into the system to break the inertia of everyone else who is playing it safe. You need to shake the status quo. You must take risks.

> You cannot please everyone; be bold where it's needed. Don't be fluffy.

Free yourself from being scared. You won't die. Take (personal) risks and be bold. Otherwise, you will get nowhere.

MAKING DECISIONS

The above inspires me to take a little detour on decision-making. Being bold, taking risks, and setting direction naturally leads me to a reflection on decision making.

There are fundamentally two types of decisions. It's essential to understand what kind of decision you are trying to make or drive.

Decisions you feel you should make and own

Get your data, understand the problem, weigh the options, and then make the decision. You are empowered to do so.

However, you cannot hide your decision. Decision authority is not a blank check to do whatever you want.

Communicate your decision out with the reasons why you took it. This is not to ask for permission, but to (1) make sure everyone is aware and (2) to let folks chime in and call out if you should have missed a key piece of data in your decision making (yes, that can happen!).

Decisions that you feel are above your paygrade, and you don't feel comfortable making them

Same as above, do the research, gather all the data, weigh all the options, prepare to the point where you would feel that you can make a decision.

Then change your communication style. Instead of communicating a decision, make a proposal, and ask for help to decide. Set a date by when you need a decision and drive to that date. Don't ask an open-ended question ('what should we do?'), don't just present alternatives without proposal and reasoning why.

In both cases of decision-making, explain the reasons for your decision or proposal. Give others the required context to follow along.

CONFIDENCE ESTABLISHES AUTHORITY

So, you have clarity on your areas of competency (and the blind spots) and work on expanding them. You freed yourself (at least partially) from being scared of mistakes and failures. You got yourself to a point where you make bold decisions and take calculated risks.

Great! Be proactive about it. You achieved a lot, project it outwards. Proactively, not just when called upon. Take the lead!

Bring it all together, and you will project competence and confidence.

Competence and confidence establish authority.

Moreover, to be clear: this is NOT the same as 'fake it until you make it.'

Go lead!

SITUATIONAL LEADERSHIP

The "Situational Leadership" framework by Ken Blanchard, is by far my favorite framework for managing and coaching people, regardless of whether it's formal or peer coaching, work or personal. You might have heard of it before. There are classes, books and of course, a Wikipedia page.

Coaching applies to all of us. As managers, we coach direct reports as part of their career development. As leaders, we coach peers to help them be more productive, overcome temporary hurdles, and to make the team better by sharing best practices. As individuals, we receive coaching and want it to be as effective as possible.

The Situational Leadership framework applies to both sides of the equation – it's a framework for leaders to give coaching, but it's also a framework for individuals to ask for more targeted support.

THE FRAMEWORK

The basic idea of the framework is that we all go through four stages of proficiency for any given skill set. It is critical to call out that this is not about our overall seniority; it is specific to the task at hand. For example, I might be extremely experienced and self–sufficient in writing specifications, but I have never done a strategy document before. I would be

D4 for specifications but D1 for strategy (see below for more explanation).

For every new task or area of competency, we go through that lifecycle of learning, from beginner to master. If we are faced with a new area, we, of course, retain mastery in the areas we already command, but we start as a rookie in the new area. Life–long learning at its best!

Situational Leadership asserts that we need different kinds of direction, coaching, and support, depending on what stage we're in <u>for that specific area and task</u>. Coaching is not one–size–fits–all but specific to the person <u>and</u> the situation.

As we make our way through new challenges, we go through four phases. See the below chart for an illustration. The lower graph is the coaching style; the upper graph is the stage an individual is in <u>for that specific task</u> (I keep underlining 'that specific task' because you screw up coaching altogether if you assess at the scope of the person, not the task).

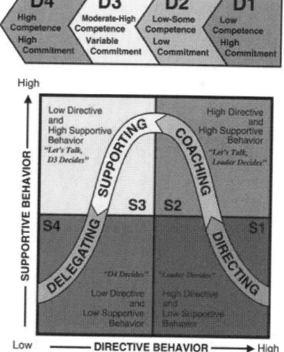

For the following discussion, I will make up my own attributes for the stages just for fun and emphasis; you can see the 'official' ones in the chart. The flow in the graph is from right to left, don't ask me why that would make any sense. You see the inverse-U-shaped flow. You can see it as a hill that you have to overcome as your motivation goes down in D2 and D3.

Stage 1: Clueless, a little scared but really motivated

> "This is awesome. However, please tell me what I should do. I'm lost."

As an individual, I just got a big new area assigned. It's fantastic, and I'm excited. However, to be honest, I'm also terrified because I don't know where to start. I feel like there is a great chance to fail, and left on my own devices, I will need to put in many hours to figure out how to approach this.

As someone who coaches, motivation is not the issue (your coachee can't yet anticipate the potential challenges ahead). There is plenty of motivation, but there also is plenty of worry as to the pure mechanics of solving the problem. In this stage, leaders need to give clear guidance on how the problem should be solved and what the specific steps and quality gates should look like. In short, provide the cookbook for solving the problem and explain what success should look like.

"Here is what you need to do. Let's meet weekly and talk about progress."

Stage 2: Got some ideas, facing early challenges

> "All right, I see what you want me to do. This is harder than I thought."

As an individual, I have made the first progress on the task. I have a plan, but things are harder than I anticipated. This starts to suck just a little bit. How can I make this easier?

This is the valley of frustration. As a leader, you need to give both moral support, but also clear guidance on how specific hurdles and blockers can be overcome. The coachee is still learning their ropes and needs guidance that they can transform into their own solutions and frameworks.

"How are things going? What's challenging? Here is what I would do in that situation."

Stage 3: Got a handle on it (mostly), not entirely smooth sailing yet

> "I think I have a plan, but let me double check with you. Things are getting a little easier."

As an individual, your confidence is increasing. You are facing problems that you have seen before, and you start having frameworks to solve them. It feels like things are becoming just a little easier lately.

The coachee is coming out of their valley of frustration. Slowly. You still need to help and support them to see the light at the end of the tunnel. They will have their own plan and solutions, which will be spot on many times, but not always. Your job becomes much more of a reviewing and tweaking role. You become a sounding board.

"Show me what you got, what's your plan? Interesting challenge, how do you plan to solve it?"

Stage 4: I know what to do, all is under control

"I got it. Get out of my way; you're slowing me down."

As an individual, you know what you need to do. You have successfully faced similar situations before. You feel confident, and since you have the frameworks in place, things now go much smoother and with less effort.

As a coach, your main job is to get out of the way and only stay informed what's going on. Give space and freedom, but be there when needed. Things are flowing for your coachee, and they are highly effective at the specific task. The item you should spend time on now is to understand what the next growth area, learning opportunity and challenge for that coachee can be and to work with them to figure out how to align new growth areas with their long–term plans. The most significant risk at this stage is for the coachee is to get bored eventually.

"Anything I should know about the project? Let's talk about what new opportunities we can prepare for you."

KEY PRINCIPLES

These are the things I believe crucial to keep in mind. It's not an official list:

- **Always make it specific to the task** – The experience model is specific to a task, not the person as a whole! Don't put the whole person into a particular bucket. If a person gets a new area they never faced before, they will likely drop back to stage 1.

- **Identifying the right stage matters** – You need to find the right level. Giving too little and too high-level coaching (directionless) is just as bad as providing too much coaching (micromanagement).

- **People move through the stages** – Watch! As you coach, people will move through levels. That's the whole point. Don't put someone in a box and leave them there. Adjust your style as the experience evolves.

- **If you're not sure, ask** – If you're not sure how much coaching someone needs, check back. Ask them, "How confident are you that you know what you need to do? Do you need any help?"

- **Get feedback** – Check in explicitly as to whether you are giving the right level of feedback. "Does that help? Is there anything else that I can help with? Do you know what to do next or do you want me to step in more?"

WHEN YOU GIVE COACHING

We all have our own leadership style. Few people naturally coach at all levels, but most of us have a preferred style that comes more natural to us. Some of us tend to be more directive and always present solutions, while others tend to be more hands–off and ask for (or assume) plans. If we don't make a conscious decision, we will fall into that style, and it will not always be the right style for the person and situation (there's a 3:1 chance it will be the wrong style).

Understand what your coachee needs for the specific task. Consciously try to identify the stage and then check back with the coachee if you're not sure. Make a mental check after the coaching session if you gave the right type of feedback and correct quickly if you didn't.

It's not about what you like to do; it's about what they need!

WHEN YOU RECEIVE COACHING

You can either hope that your manager, coach, or mentor knows what you need, or you can tell them. I would do the latter. See where they go, but if you feel you're still unclear what to do or you feel over–managed, tell them! "Can you give me a little more guidance, I don't know where to start on this?" or, in the other case, "I think I have a plan. Let me work on it, and we'll review it together in two days."

Don't leave it to the coach; be specific. If your coach makes the right assessment, excellent. If not, clarify and help them. Likewise, if you feel you have moved on to the next stage, let your coach know that you would like the type of feedback to change.

Needing more direction for a new challenge is not a bad thing at all. Not articulating it and then falling behind is.

Situational Leadership requires a little more work. However, the impact is astounding.

KEEP HEADING TOWARDS YOUR BIG AND DAUNTING GOALS

D o you know where you want to be in a year, in 5 years, in 10 years? Do you know what you want to achieve in your life? Do you know what you want to proudly look back at when it's time to make the big tally?

Know where you want to go and keep your goal in focus. Find opportunities to celebrate and award yourself along the way. Suck it up if times are tough, but also be gentle and forgiving to yourself – not everything will always work out exactly as you thought.

I hope you don't just idle along from day to day, getting blown around by the random winds of life.

KNOW YOUR GOALS

It all starts with knowing where you want to go. Don't merely think about the next step you could do from where you are. Think about where you want to be when all is said and done. Then work backwards from that end goal and lay out the path that gets you there.

Think long-term. Prepare, invest, and build for your future. Don't fall prey to the easy way out or the instant gratification. Keep your eyes on the goal post.

FIND LITTLE REWARDS ON THE WAY

When you have a goal that's a little out there and maybe even daunting, it's crucial to find and set rewards along the way.

Do what engaging games are doing: establish small goals and rewards along the way. Celebrate when you achieve those milestones. Keep yourself moving to your distant end goal by setting in–between goals that you reach along the way. Set rewards with those goals that keep you excited and keep you going.

TRAIN YOUR RESILIENCE

Sometimes, probably many times, it will be hard to push to your goal. There will be many temptations to go the easier way that provides instant gratification but distracts you from your desired outcome (e.g., plunking down in front of the TV instead of going for a run).

Here are some things you can do when 'the going gets tough':

- **Look forward** – keep your goal in mind, keep the forward momentum in focus
- **Get perspective** – put things into perspective, don't get stuck in the current feeling but look at the bigger picture
- **Know your why** – be clear with yourself why you are doing things, what drives you
- **Build on your passion** – find the opportunities in the current moment or the challenging situation that you are passionate about, spend as much time as you can on those

THE RULE OF 80:20

While all of the above is true and good, sometimes life happens. If you head towards your goals 80% of the time, you can be proud of yourself. If you strive for 100%, you will get hard, myopic and will probably miss out on a bunch of equally important things.

Always remember:

The art lies in the empty space.

Give yourself some slack every now and then. Be focused but also let go when the pressure builds up too much. Even the most robust tank needs a pressure valve.

Be focused but also let go. Don't force yourself too much. Take a day off. Forget all your rules and duties, put down this guide, and enjoy life for at least one day the week.

LIVING IS LEARNING

I was reading "Mastery" by Robert Green and one of the things that stuck out for me was how Robert stressed the importance of the 'apprenticeship phase' before creativity and mastery can be reached. It reminded me of key lessons I learned early (and unconsciously) through martial arts practice.

However, reflecting a little more, I would suggest the learning mindset should never change and what one should genuinely develop is a 'lifelong apprentice mindset.'

NEVER STOP LEARNING NEW AREAS

Everyone talks about lifelong learning today. Most people think about deepening their subject area expertise when they do. I believe there is a more significant opportunity hidden in expanding into entirely new areas.

Robert Greene has some such examples in his book as well, as he discusses people who went through multiple different apprenticeships over the time of their life, finally merging those skills to understand underlying principles better or to develop entirely new areas.

The most compelling opportunity that learning new areas opens up is the fact that the spectrum of things you can do widens instead of shrinking. If your focus is on getting better and better at one single thing, you face a good chance of either that thing becoming obsolete in the future or someone else outcompeting you in that narrowly scoped area. If you learn to do many things well, then your horizon of opportunities keeps expanding through your life as you mix those abilities into new compelling portfolios.

I learned this in martial arts, studying diverse disciplines and with that enhancing my core style. Looking back, it rubbed off on my approach to professional life as well, where over the years I pursued experiences in coding, marketing, business development, PR, product management, and teaching.

LEARN TO LOVE PAIN AND FRUSTRATION

Robert Greene mentions this as well: you must learn to embrace and seek learning experiences that are painful and frustrating. If you don't focus on the things that are hardest for you (and thus most painful and frustrating), then you won't learn the traits of your trade that you are deficient in and will never truly master the area.

It's way too easy to focus on the easy wins and the things that you're good at. I am guilty of that too. However, only playing to your strengths will prevent you from expanding the scope of your abilities. While leading to quicker wins in the short-term, it will limit your ability to master an area long-term since you will never close those capability gaps.

Martial arts teaches through pain, sweat, and tears. For good schools that's figuratively rather than literally (maybe except the sweat part). However, they make you continuously face your most significant challenges and learn to overcome them. I think the same is true for our professional development, only with the big difference that it's usually up to you to push yourself beyond your limits. Business often offers you an easy way out until the day when it's too late to change. You need to be pushing yourself.

- **Never stop learning** – Never think you 'know it'.
- **Disrupt yourself** – When you feel like you've reached a comfortable level in mastering an area, then it's time to disrupt yourself and move on to something entirely different.
- **Face the challenges** – Focus on learning the skills that are hard for you. You will learn the things that align with your strengths anyway. As to learning time, your knowledge gaps are what needs the most attention.

BE DELIBERATE ABOUT YOUR GROWTH

I wanted to share how I think about career development in general but also specifically at Amazon. Take it as what it is, my personal view. However, to go with Colin Powell: "It worked for me."

GROW YOUR EQUITY

Invest in yourself!

In my mind, career growth is primarily about how you invest in yourself. It's about what new skills you can learn what new experiences you can gain. It's about how you can expand the scope of your impact as you get better at what you do.

You can think about it through the lens of a job interview. We all do plenty of those as interviewers. What stories from candidates excite us? What stories can you tell and what do you need to do to expand the set of exciting stories about your professional life. Your career growth plan is how you build up the examples that will excite other people and yourself. As experienced interviewers, we know that it's never about the title a candidate brings, but it's always about how they solved complex problems and overcame challenging headwinds in creative and inclusive ways.

PROMOTION IS A BY-PRODUCT OF CAREER GROWTH

> Career growth doesn't equal promotion. Promotion is a by-product of career growth.

At Amazon, we deliberately only have a few levels. Therefore, the time between promotions is longer than in many other companies, and the difference between levels is larger. However, the growth opportunities in a level are plenty and will allow you to build the anecdotes and data to prove that you are ready for the next step when you are ready.

Looking back to a previous life that seems far away, I remember that at Microsoft, we plopped from level 63 to 64 to 65 every two years. There was lots of instant gratification, but it was also somehow meaningless since, in most cases, the job title didn't even change. At Amazon, we take big deliberate steps with more extended personal growth periods in between. The scope, responsibility, and impact we are given as individuals during those growth periods are mind-blowing in comparison to other companies.

KNOW WHERE YOU WANT TO GO AND START BEING THAT PERSON TODAY

> Where do you want to be in 2–3 years?

Be clear in your mind what you want to do in 2 or 3 years. Understand how you will operate in that role. Look at people who are already performing in that role or at that level and know what they do differently from you. Then look for opportunities to do the same. Work in the same way (the 'how' much more than the 'what'). Talk to your manager and make sure she knows where you want to go, can provide you with proper opportunities and give you relevant coaching and feedback along the way.

Seek opportunities to learn how those role models do what they do and then find ways for yourself to show similar behaviors and outcomes (don't just copy them, nothing is more depressing than a bad copy). Deliver at that quality bar consistently, and people will notice. Once enough people notice, you will get promoted.

For example, a promotion at Amazon is not a bet of leadership that you might eventually be able to grow into a new level. We don't follow the Peter principle (i.e., you get promoted until you fail in your level). At Amazon, we promote people who already perform at the next level. We promote once people have consistently demonstrated that they are ready. Promotion at Amazon is an acknowledgment that you already have what it takes, not that we have high hopes that you might eventually get there.

MAKE PERSONAL GROWTH GOALS

Make a plan, be clear, be deliberate, and understand what the bar is.

What is it that you want to work on? What scope do you want to expand in? Where can you help your organization? What things can you take to the next level to role-model for the rest of your team?

Understand where you want to go. Understand what the expectations are for that role and level. Understand where you need to add to your existing experiences (regular career discussions are an excellent tool for that). Make a plan!

Those plans don't need to be tied to a next level though (in my mind in most cases they shouldn't). I'm coming back to my first and most crucial point – <u>it's about how you grow your skills and equity</u>. For example, for me, I wanted to widen my focus and impact beyond my direct PM team. I made it a goal for this year to find ways to help coach the broader org so that we can all be more productive and fulfilled. Will I learn a lot? For sure! Will that get me promoted to Director? No way. Do I worry much about that? Not a minute. It's a ton of fun, and I learn many new things along the way.

WHERE MY MARTIAL ARTS AND MY BUSINESS SELF MEETS

I have three big passions in my life: family, martial arts, and growing people and teams. While following each of those passions, I learned that universal principles apply, and each of those have cross-pollinated the other areas heavily.

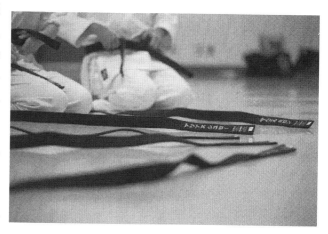

I've been doing martial arts for over 25 years now. Here are some of my principles that came over from that area into my leadership toolbox. None of the following is breathtakingly net–new (yes, you can stop reading now if you were hoping for that) but it's a framework that makes it easier for me to remember the key learnings.

> Do it fully or don't do it at all. If you go in, give it your all. However, always stay open-minded and flexible. Water breaks the rock.

DO IT OR DON'T DO IT, BUT DON'T DO IT HALF-HEARTED

Be in the moment

Being in the moment is a critical principle in martial arts, Zen, and meditation. It's about focusing on the now and not getting distracted by what has been or what might be in the future.

This is extremely powerful for being effective in business as well. Focus on the task at hand and nothing else. Turn off notifications, put away your phone, and hide your email inbox. Moreover, come back to enjoy those distractions once you've accomplished your task.

It's also super important as you interact with people. Listening skills are a highly valued skill today, mostly because many people cannot focus on what the person sitting in front of them is trying to tell them. Stop playing with your phone or thinking about your smart answer that you will provide in response. Just listen to the person and show her that you do. Your partnership will improve tremendously!

It's all or nothing

In martial arts, if you engage, you engage. No matter what the consequences are, you already decided that it is critical to engage. Moreover, you will pull it through.

I've learned that in business, we're often too afraid of losing to do what it takes to succeed. I was most successful when we had no kids, two incomes, and I didn't care whether I would lose my job over bold decisions.

I love my job and want to keep it, and I need to feed a family now, but I do try to remind myself that you need to be willing to lose (everything) to make the bold decisions that are required to be successful.

If you think it is important enough to do it, do it all the way. My teacher used to say, "there is no being half pregnant."

THINGS CHANGE, DON'T MISS THE OPPORTUNITY

Stay flexible

Be smart though. Things will change as you move along. The initial plan that you want to follow through badly might not be appropriate anymore. Keep your focus on the goal but don't get stubborn on your execution plan.

In martial arts, your partner seldom tends to react the way you think she should have reacted. Stay flexible, stay on your toes, and shift your execution as your parameters change.

Avoid blind spots

To stay flexible, you need first to know what's going on and recognize if situations change. In martial arts, we talk a lot about tunnel vision, the effect where you focus so much on one partner that you don't even see as the other one approaches you from behind.

Maintain 360-degree vision. You need to stay on top of what's going on in your industry and area of expertise as well as the broader initiatives in your company.

However, you should extend your 360-degree awareness beyond business opportunities to your relationship with people. Are you deeply tuned into how people interact with you and how they react to you? Are you making it a point to reflect on how you appear to people, what your behavior and your style projects? Do you observe how team members perceive your posture and even your dress style when they interact with you (i.e., do you send the signal that you value them as a partner and thus care about the impression you make on them)? Do you behave in employee 1:1s the way you would in an interview or a board meeting?

Keep it simple

In martial arts, the final mastery is to leave out everything that is not necessary. Slow is smooth, smooth is fast. If you leave everything out that is not necessary, then the remaining is 100% effective (and yes, no one ever gets there).

In your work, simplify to be able to adapt faster. Process and complexity keep creeping up. Entropy will finally win (so much I remember from my physics master) but your job in life is to fight it.

Keep the mindset to continually improve what's needed but don't be afraid to cut the rest. Focus on a few things and do them right (reminder: by definition focus does mean you can't do everything).

IT'S A JOURNEY, NOT A DESTINATION

Always remember that you're in for the long run. You better make sure you make it all the way to the finish line and won't drop out before. In martial arts, if you make an impressive first move but then go down badly you won't get many cheers (or feel great about it afterward).

Be balanced

If you're the world's most excellent jump kicker, someday a fellow will come along and wrestle you to the mat. If you never thought about wrestling before, you will feel very miserable down there.

Keep up your motivation by following and nurturing your passions (and by making sure that you have more than one passion). Sometimes things will go awesome in one area, but sometimes it might be bumpy – in those situations, it's great to have a second source to pull motivation and energy from. It's devastating if the only thing that defined you goes through an extended slow patch.

Don't be a one trick pony; they get burned out quickly. Don't neglect the things that are important to you. Balance your time across work, relationships, and hobbies. Have all three of them!

A healthy mind in a healthy body

There is a Latin proverb for that. However, I didn't take Latin in school and better not pretend to have any such skills.

The concept is easy, though: you live in your body. Every day. That makes it your most important tool of all, please don't break it.

Get the sleep you need (find out how much that is and then be religious about it). Do sports. You don't have to run a marathon. Find out what works for you and build a habit around it.

Pace yourself! At times you have to outperform everyone else. It feels great to do so! However, then there needs to be a time where you turn it down a notch and recharge your batteries. Pace yourself to be ready when ready is required. Don't burn all your energy before the race starts. Take your long and short breaks.

Never stop being a student

In martial arts, you never end being a student. In fact, once you stop learning, you start losing. It is just the same in life.

Be humble but aspirational and keep a learning mindset. Keep learning and keep stretching yourself; that's the most fun part of life!

If you draw a short and a long line on the ground, there are two ways to make the long line shorter. Most people try to wash some away from the long line, to erase it. That's hard and messy and generally much work which more often than not fails. A lot of competitive strategies work that way today where one competitor tries to throw rocks in the other ones way. A much easier way is actually to extend the short line. Invest in your abilities and leave the competition behind.

FINAL THOUGHT

In martial arts, once it's done, it's done. You can learn from the many mistakes you just made but you can't change any of them anymore – they're out the door. You also don't wallow in the past since it's meaningless.

ONCE YOU STOP GROWING YOU START DECLINING

NEVER STOP LEARNING AND GROWING!

Once you stop growing, you start declining.

Never stop observing, learning, tweaking, optimizing and improving yourself and how you live your life.

Life is a marathon, not a sprint. It's the path we take and the choices we make that count, not any singular goal that we are heading out for.

At the end, what matters are not the possessions that you've accumulated, but the learnings you had and the person you became. It's about how you improved yourself and what you left behind.

Never think that you are too old for something new. Never assume that you are 'there.' Once you stop learning, growing and pushing, you start declining. You start to crumble and die.

There is not much steady state in life. It's either up or down. There is also no rule in life or the universe that says you cannot go up and grow until the very end. As a matter of fact, that is precisely what Chinese medicine and Tai Chi try to achieve: live healthy as long as you can and grow until the end. Set your sights high up all the way through.

Back in Germany I all too often saw successful people retire at age 60, stop doing anything and then rapidly falling apart. Don't do that to yourself – at any age. Keep the learner's mindset, be a lifelong apprentice.

No matter where you are, what your circumstances are, and where you will go next, you can always make yourself just a little bit better. You can always make your life a little more balanced and meaningful. You can always strive to become an even better person.

The path is the reward, not the destination.

THE FOUR BURNERS

I read an interesting article about work-life balance, "The Downside of Work-Life Balance" by James Clear.

THE THEORY

The theory is that you can compare juggling your life with four burners. One for Family, one for health, one for friends and one for career (you might notice that I sorted and prioritized them differently from James).

The statement then is that to be successful, you have to cut down one burner so you can focus on the others. To be really successful, you have to cut down two burners.

James talks about various strategies you can apply to get there. I see a core of truth and value in most of them, but I think they are also each similarly dangerous for a balanced life.

LIFE HAS SEASONS

The strategy that comes closest to something that makes sense to me is the 'seasonal strategy' – you focus on different things in different life stages. That does make sense; you want to set priorities as you go through life. When you start a new career, focus on learning, when you have kids, focus on raising them well.

Where is disagree is the assumption that you should focus entirely during those times. What good are a high paying job and a great career if you don't live long enough to enjoy the fruits? How much is your wealth worth if your kids don't talk to you anymore when you're old and seeking company? How useful is that dream body if you don't have friends?

SEEK A BALANCED LIFE BUT SET FOCUS POINTS

My point here is that the key is a balanced life. Yes, it is! Work-life balance got a bad vibe in recent years with our gig economy and always–on mentality. You need to balance though! You need to invest in the long–term!

You can make the seasonal model work if you pick a few constraints:

- **Family** – Never compromise on the family. Ever. Really.
- **Health** – Have a baseline for health. Don't go below it. You might not need to train for Iron Man every year, but you do want to live to your retirement.
- **Career** – Double down on career growth when the return is right. Change your career when it isn't. However, doubling down needs to come with a timeline. You cannot double down for 30 years. Treat it like a marathon with deliberate sprints in between.
- **Friends** – The friends that truly matter. They will understand if you have times when you're busy and need to focus on other things. Just explain it to them. They will wait for you.

Never compromise on the family. Never go under a baseline for health Adjust the rest with a clear focused plan.

Yes, it's four burners. However, if you turn any of them down too much for too long of a time, your meal will go bad before you can serve it.

> Life is not a sprint. Life is a marathon with sprints in between.

CLOSING THOUGHTS

ENJOYED THIS BOOK? WRITE A REVIEW!

If you've enjoyed this book, the best compliment you can give is writing a review. As self-published authors, we don't have the advertising power of a major publishing firm.

However, you can make a big difference. Honest reviews help other readers find us. It only takes five minutes, and the review can be as short as you like.

If you'd like to leave a review online, search for this book on Amazon and click on reviews.

Thank you very much, truly appreciated.

GOOD READS

There are countless great books on business and (self-) management. I cannot possibly list all that inspired me over the years. Below is a short list of the ones I read recently and found relevant to the topics in this book. Enjoy!

ESTABLISHING HABITS

Mini Habits: Smaller Habits, Bigger Results
Stephen Guise
ISBN–10: 1494882272

A quick and straightforward guide on developing small habits and let them grow to bigger ones over time.

Atomic Habits: Tiny Changes, Remarkable Results
James Clear
ISBN–10: 1847941834

Lots of good advice on developing habits. It also shares some of the science behind habit forming and how to go further. "Change your self–image instead of chasing goals!"

FOCUSING ON WHAT MATTERS

The ONE Thing: The Surprisingly Simple Truth Behind Extraordinary Results
Gary Keller, Jay Papasan
ISBN–10: 1848549253

Stay focused on the one thing you need to achieve. There is always one thing that's more important than anything else. What's your one thing today, this week, this year?

Willpower: Rediscovering the Greatest Human Strength
Roy Baumeister, John Tierney
ISBN–10: 0143122231

Besides time, willpower is your most valuable resource. Learn what depletes willpower and what you can do to preserve it to get the most out of it.

Off the Clock: Feel Less Busy While Getting More Done
Laura Vanderkam
ISBN–10: 0735219818

Lots of good advice. My favorite one is on making experiences a priority. "Plan it in. Do it anyway."

LIVING WITHIN YOUR VALUES

Dark Horse: Achieving Success Through the Pursuit of Fulfillment
Todd Rose, Ogi Ogas
ISBN–10: 0062931547

There are many ways to be successful, find what YOU want to do. Not what others tell you or do.

An Audience of One: Reclaiming Creativity for Its Own Sake
Srinivas Rao, Robin Dellabough
ISBN–10: 1101981733

Your pursuit for passion or art is about you, no one else. Don't try to please others. Don't chase external confirmation. Do it for yourself.

Conscious Business
Fred Kofman
ISBN–10: 1622032020

A little lengthy but the book presents sound principles on how to live and do business by your values and with integrity. It also tells a great side story on accountability culture.

CHANGING YOUR SELF–PERCEPTION

Presence: Bringing Your Boldest Self to Your Biggest Challenges
Amy Cuddy
ISBN–10: 0316256587

Harvard scientists have proven what martial arts taught for centuries: "Your inside reflects on your outside, your outside reflects on your inside."

The Happiness Advantage: The Seven Principles of Positive Psychology That Fuel Success and Performance at Work
Shawn Achor
ISBN–10: 9780753539477

Success comes from happiness, not the other way around. The stories you tell yourself define your perspective, which in turn determines your happiness level. Learn to be happy.

MORE BOOKS FROM THE AUTHORS

Finding the Heart – Our first book explores and explains basic principles (the 'heart') for Tai Chi and life that we learned through our martial arts journey from some of the best teachers in their fields.

Alfons and Ulrike Staerk
ISBN-10: 1724173685

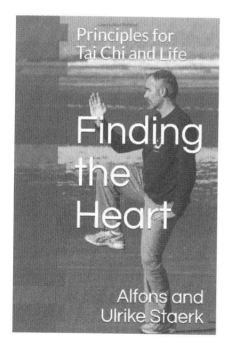

In Closing

Thank you for reading this book and following our thoughts.

We would love to hear from you! You can send us a message through our website www.KeruUmaBudo.com or sign up for our mailing list from there. You can follow our blog on KeruUmaBudo.wordpress.com.

Consider leaving a review on Amazon. Share if you liked the book; let us know how we can improve if you didn't.

Made in the USA
Middletown, DE
14 September 2019